BE TH(
MY BREAS

BE THOU
MY BREASTPLATE

*Forty Days of Giving
your Life to God the Celtic Way*

Paul Wallis

mowbray

Mowbray

The Tower Building
11 York Road
London SE1 7NX

Suite 704, 80 Maiden Lane
New York
NY 10010

www.continuumbooks.com

First published 2008

British Library Cataloguing-in-Publication Data
A catalogue record for this book is available from the British Library.
ISBN 9781906286194
Designed and typeset by Benn Linfield
Printed and bound by MPG Books, Cornwall, United Kingdom

Contents

The Breastplate of Fursa

How to pray this Breastplate Prayer

Forty individual prayers and meditations

Appendix 1 – Lent with Fursa

Appendix 2 – Weekend retreat with Fursa

To my beautiful and wonderful wife, Ruth

The Breastplate of Fursa

May the yoke of the Law of God be upon this shoulder,
The coming of the Holy Spirit on this head,
The sign of Christ on this forehead,
The hearing of the Holy Spirit in these ears,
The smelling of the Holy Spirit in this nose.
The vision that the people of heaven have be in these eyes,
The speech of the people of heaven in this mouth,
The work of the Church of God in these hands
The good of God and of neighbour in these feet.
May God dwell in this heart,
And this person belong entirely to God the Father.

How to pray this Breastplate Prayer

The ancient Celtic Christians had a uniquely powerful way of giving their lives to God. It was called the Breastplate Prayer (or Lorica). As the name implies, it was a prayer invoking God's blessing and protection on the life of the one who prayed it. Symbolically the ancient Celts would use such a prayer to rededicate to God every part of their physical body and every aspect of their daily life. A few of these prayers, so loved by our spiritual ancestors, have survived to this day. One of the most powerful was the Breastplate of Fursa.

Its author, Fursa, was an evangelist, church planter and founder of monastic communities in Ireland, England and France. History records that he penned these 11 brief lines of prayer some time in the early seventh century. Today his prayer is still powerful. It has lost none of its resonance. I know this because some years ago I prayed this prayer over the airwaves on BBC Radio in the UK as part of one of their 'God slots'. I soon discovered that Fursa's words had reached out and touched people in a way that the many words of my own spoken through countless other broadcasts had never done. I knew this because all of a sudden there came a flood of letters and calls from people all around the country and beyond, all anxious to get hold of this obscure Celtic prayer. The response was huge because Fursa's words resonated so powerfully with their new contemporary audience.

The resonant words of Fursa's prayer have stayed with me, too. Whether on retreat with others or praying alone in private I often turn to this special prayer because it so powerfully expresses the prayers and longing of many hearts – including my own. Somehow, when things seem complicated, confusing or distracting, Fursa's prayer brings me back to the simplicity of the Gospel of Jesus Christ.

But why should that be so? What is it that has given these 11 succinct lines such a long-lasting power? How is it that Fursa's Breastplate has been able to span these 14 centuries, is still able to move and inspire people, and can still speak for women and men seeking God in their lives?

This way of giving oneself to God differs from the one-off exercise of the classic 'sinner's prayer', which first introduced me to the Kingdom of God. The Breastplate Prayer can certainly be used that way – as a point of entrance into the walk of faith. Back in the seventh century, however, the Breastplate Prayer was used by the ancient Celtic Christians as a personal act of devotion to be spoken from memory by the individual believer with the beginning of each and every new day. Just as the Apostle Paul tells the Christians hearing the letter of the Ephesians that they should habitually 'put on' the helmet of salvation, the belt of truth and the shield of faith, so in the same way a lorica invites those making the prayer to remember all that God has given them and clothe themselves in the blessings of their relationship with God.

Fursa's prayer is one of a number of Breastplate prayers from that distant time in history. Mary Byrne and Eleanor Hull's inspiring hymn 'Be Thou my Vision' (from which this book takes its title) was based on the most familiar of Breastplate Prayers – the Breastplate of St Patrick. Fursa's prayer goes beyond that hymn's wonderful vision of God's protection, by dedicating to God every part of the believer's body. Symbolically his prayer pledges a total dedication to the purposes of God and invites a total immersion in the life of God. But a Breastplate prayer is far more than a symbolic act. It moves in at least three dimensions. It is a physical act; it is an act of speech and it is an act of imagination. I have found this three-dimensional kind of praying to be especially powerful in the seasons when I feel particularly two-dimensional: those periods when we feel emotionally flat, spiritually shallow or physically deflated. I mean those times of disengagement when our own words of prayer seem merely to dribble off our lips, leaving us feeling not only unchanged but further depressed and bored by the lameness of our own Godward speaking. In these times especially, this ancient Celtic tool comes into its own.

Maybe praying a prayer penned by another person is an unfamiliar practice for you. If so, then think of it as being no different from speaking a psalm of praise by David or singing a great hymn of worship by Charles Wesley. Use it that way, as a spoken hymn. To make such words sincere and truly our own, the first and essential thing is to find words with which we profoundly agree. Only then can such words speak for us and offer to God the sincere prayer of our own hearts. Remember that the words do not create your prayer: they express it. A prayer is not like a spell in which the words have to be exactly right in order to create the magic. Words of prayer do not create the Christian's connection with God: the Risen Christ does, the moment we put our faith in him. What words of prayer do is help us enter into this Christ-given relationship with God.

So when you begin using Fursa's Breastplate as part of your daily discipline, don't approach it as if the goal is to create an atmosphere or to make something happen. Simply speak each word and verse, slowly and out loud, picturing the meaning of each word and phrase as you speak it, perhaps sensing or touching each part of the body as it is named and re-offered to God. The sincerity of this prayer is not measured by any feelings it generates, but by our own agreement with what we are saying – the agreement of intention and action.

To pray Fursa's Breastplate aloud, slowly and thought-fully, need take no longer than one minute. This makes it a very user-friendly exercise, able to find a niche in even the most frenetic of schedules. In this book, I will invite you to pray Fursa's prayer each morning. But I will ask you to do a little more than that. Each day's chapter will invite you to return to one line or phrase and then together we will explore some of the meaning and significance of what this prayer has invited you to do and say.

At the beginning of the 40 days your engagement with the prayer will be simply at the level of agreement. However, by the end of this book you will find that your mind has anchored to each word and verse a whole body of thoughts and feelings. Together our minds will have filled the words of the prayer with imaginative associations and theological reflections. By day 40 you will find that, almost on their own, the words of Fursa's prayer will evoke as you speak them a broader and deeper consciousness of the miracle in which you stand: the presence of Almighty God. This is the way a Breastplate Prayer can work, daily building that awareness of God in the one who prays it. By day 40 it will take you rather longer than a minute to pray Fursa's prayer. And you will want it to!

The Apostle Paul exhorts me as a believer to clothe myself in the armour of God in order that I might be more conscious of what I am doing as I take my stand 'in the strength of the Lord and in the power of his might'. This is my prayer for you as you embark on this 40-day journey with Fursa. By the end of the journey you will have entered a little into Fursa's story and caught some glimpses of his world as we have it sketched by ancient historians. But more importantly than that, let the prayer engage you in your own world with more heart and soul and a greater joy in knowing the closer-than-your-own-breath presence of God.

There are, of course, many ways of strengthening an obedient and prayerful relationship with God. The intention of this little book is simply to guide you through 40 days of doing that in the way it was done 14 centuries ago; in a time when Christianity was much younger, more spontaneous, less organized and certainly less institutionalized than today. For these reasons, it has a strong appeal for the postmodern believer. This was the way followed by an evangelist and church planter who bore incredible fruit through the way he lived for God. May you be blessed as you give yourself afresh to our life-giving God in this ancient, Celtic way.

Forty individual prayers
and meditations

Day One

'May the yoke of the Law of God be upon this shoulder'

Of all the things mankind has made, few inventions have ever surpassed the phenomenal importance of the humble yoke. Think of it: in the time before the yoke our distant ancestor was able to plough just enough land for himself. With an animal and a plough, perhaps this man could farm just enough for his family to make a living from their humble little strip of land. Bear in mind that if the family ever outgrew the men's ability to farm, the family would become scattered – its members disconnected from the land and dispersed to a life of serving others as serfs or wandering the country as nomads. Thus scattered, the family's ownership of and connection with the land would be severed and in those distant days such a serious mis-fortune would leave them one critical link further down the social food chain.

But the invention of the yoke enabled our ancestor to subdue and farm an area maybe ten times the size of his former little strip of land. With co-operation, a small cluster of families with a pair of oxen, an iron plough and a yoke to share among them, would be able to live at a much higher level. Now they could eat enough to grow bigger and stronger, to be fruitful and multiply in number. Aided by the yoke, our ancestors could cultivate enough to store for uncertain times ahead, the more surely to survive any lean years to come, and also to enter into trade with their neighbours.

With the coming of the yoke the family can become a tribe, the tribe a trading post and the trading post a township, where people can specialize according to their gifts and so enrich the whole life of the community.

It is strange but true mathematics that when two beasts are yoked together their effectiveness is more than doubled. An ox-master can set his sights on higher goals and a better life.

When Fursa first prayed to be yoked with the Law of God, he was praying that through Christ's Law – His words and ways – he would become connected together with God in a fruitful partnership of common purpose. He knew that without God maybe he could just survive (though not outlast) his poor earthly life, but that tied shoulder-to-shoulder with God he could live on an entirely different level. Yoked with God he could set his sights on higher goals and a better life, the abundant life of Christ. Daily accepting God's yoke through the words of this lorica, its earliest speakers would more consciously remember the sweetness of their attachment to God's earth and the joy of working in connection with heaven. Fursa's prayer begins by calling out to God for this connection to be made real.

A Breastplate Prayer is intended as a daily act of self-offering, so Fursa's prayer is extremely democratic. What I mean is that it does nothing to discriminate between the person who has been a believer in Christ for 30 years and the one who has been a believer for 30 minutes. It simply offers a form of words to anyone who would look to God and say 'God be near to me', 'God be bound to me', 'I offer you my shoulders'.

So, whatever your age or stage in the journey of faith, if you have lately felt unconnected with God or ineffective, lacking in purpose, or sensing that you are merely eking out a life that is too bare and shallow, then Fursa's prayer begins with words to express your fundamental heart cry. If you are hungry for a sense of meaning, desperate to bear some fruit and multiply, or wanting in whatever way to raise your sights to something better, then take your stand with Fursa and cry out for the yoke of the Law of God to rest on your shoulder.

Day Two

'May the yoke of the Law of God be upon this shoulder'

The yoke's technology is simple yet profound. The rigid strength of a two-oxen yoke ensures that the power of both animals is harnessed for, if one beast outpaces the other, the faster ox soon realizes that it is bearing the burden of the whole load. The ox-master would quickly sense it too because his machine would lose power. Not only would the farmer find he was ploughing with the power of a single ox but that animal's power would itself be diminished by the added burden of having to drag, along with the plough, the dawdling second beast. This would be painful for the leading ox and a loss to the ox-master. But this inequality of labour would be painful too to the slower ox, for its shoulder would be chafed and bruised by the heaving of the heavy yoke continually yanking its shoulders forwards. That is why Saint Paul warns us not to be 'unequally yoked' ourselves. With a little human tuition the simple bovine brains learned that if they walked the same way and worked at equal speed the labour would seem only half as heavy – not burdensome but easy and light.

Likewise, when Jesus calls to women and men, saying 'Take my yoke upon you and learn from me . . . my yoke is easy and my burden light', he is calling us to walk his way and to walk at his pace. If we heed his call, choosing his way and pace, then the furrow we plough will be a journey heavenwards and the burden shared with our mighty Saviour. The connection Jesus calls for is also a strong and a rigid one. Fursa's prayer reminds us that our link with Christ is through the 'Law of God' – the gift of Christ's teaching and commands. 'No-one who sets his shoulder to the plough and looks back is worthy of me', said the Son of Mary.

Fursa does not ask for some vague, elastic kind of relationship, but for something strong and binding. This is a relationship intended not to add demands to the burdens of life but rather to define the direction, lessen the burden and increase the fruit.

Fursa lived his life in the truth of these words. His building, farming, preaching, recruiting, pastoring and travelling from Ireland to England and from England to France left in its wake stable and strong missionary communities. To establish such order requires the expenditure of great effort and energy. And yet his story does not read like a litany of arduous labours and toil. As recorded by Bede and others, Fursa was one who seemed to lead his life at walking pace, unhurried yet effective and always in close tandem with the giver of all purpose and fruit – his heavenly yoke-mate, paraclete and Master.

If you ever feel weary and fruitless in your 'toilsome labour under the sun', whatever it is your work may be; if you long for that sense of finding your groove and taking all life in your stride, then simply pray and ask for what

Fursa sought from Christ. With the words of his prayer, call out for the divine technology of the yoke of the law of God, inviting it now to rest upon your own shoulder.

Day Three

'May the yoke of the Law of God be upon this shoulder'

Our Celtic forefathers knew the patterns of tides and seasons. Their lives were wrapped up in the repeating cycles of seedtime and harvest, morning and evening, birth and death. Yet we know from the gathered prayers of various Celtic people-groups that these island Christians were not believers in a relentless, unchangeable inevitability. They knew that life events might have different outcomes: a harvest might succeed or fail; an illness might end in death or life; a family might prosper or fall; a pagan king might resist the Gospel or convert to Christ.

Like most monastic pioneers in history, Fursa was a farmer. Now, any farmer can tell you that when left to God alone, a farm doesn't do too well. It doesn't sow itself, tend its own livestock or reap itself. It is only when human effort and God's blessing are combined that the result is crops rather than weeds, healthy livestock rather than sick, and harvests rather than chaos. In the 'self-sufficient' life of a monastery farm, the effort of men and the blessing of God are both essential.

Fursa and the communities of young men he recruited and with whom he shared his life knew this truth very well. Every little community that Fursa gathered began its life in this same way, each brother building his own simple dry-stone or wooden cell, and those cells clustering around a central stone chapel. On their land the brothers then ran the livestock and cultivated the crops on which they relied for food and materials. As farmers, they understood that they depended both on the grace of God and the fruit of their own labour in order to prosper. To the minds of such believers there was therefore no contradiction between the sovereignty of God and the necessity of our own efforts.

Celtic prayers are built largely on that belief, grounded in the reality of a farmer's life, that divine and human action could each alter the outcomes of life. That is why, in addressing the many uncertainties of daily living, Celtic prayers call upon Almighty God for his sovereign power and help, not neglecting to give back to God whatever work and endeavour the one making the prayer might be able to offer.

Praying Fursa's prayer and taking on the yoke of Christ, the believer now chooses to offer his or her own shoulder – all in the belief that, when harnessed with Christ, we can and must labour towards good results. Fursa's, then, is unmistakably an active spirituality.

Years ago I knew a man who was insistent that he wanted nothing to do with the Gospel of Christ. This, he told me, was because he did not want to be told that the way things are in this poor world is simply the will of God.

'The rich man in his castle, the poor man at his gate,
God made them high or lowly, he ordered their estate.'

My friend had heard this preached and had rejected it.

Rather than submit to the injustices of this world, he wanted to right wrongs, help the needy, bring healing to the sick, food to the hungry and release to the oppressed. Then one day he heard the call of Christ expressed in exactly those terms. For the first time he understood the Messiah to be issuing a recruiting call to join with God in fighting for all those things he believed were right. When my friend heard this, his heart was touched and he gave his life to God – heart, soul, mind and strength.

Such was the faith of Fursa who, from his twenties onwards, gave a lifetime of effort to preaching the Gospel, forming group-houses, founding monasteries and chapels, and to touching many lives with the saving and healing power of the holy name of Jesus. The fruit, so Bede tells us, was the conversion 'of many unbelievers to Christ'.

Fursa's spirituality, then, was not about tranquil submission to some imagined, inevitable, what-will-be-will-be divine will but rather consisted chiefly in a taking of personal responsibility for the apostolic commission of Christ. The passion of this faith is shown in his steady life-long devotion to following the ways of God.

So it is that the words of Fursa's prayer call upon the one who prays them to devote themselves to God, and lend their own shoulder to the cause and purposes of Christ. If your heart's desire is to make yourself a part of Christ's answer to the questions and problems of this world, then simply pray with Fursa for the yoke of the Law of God to rest upon your shoulder.

Day Four

'May the yoke of the Law of God be upon this shoulder'

Somewhere deep in the heart of every person is the long-ing for a sense of purpose. It is something primordial to our human nature to thirst for some feeling of greater significance. To be born and then die without leaving any mark somehow seems to fall short of what we were made for.

'The Lord God placed Adam in the garden for him to work it', says the book of Genesis.

The special word for work that the writer employs in that ancient Hebrew sentence conveys 'something to accom-plish or pursue'. The Lord God knew that to be happy the man needed something to achieve or to reach for. Every person since Adam has felt the same need.

The Messiah himself once told his disciples: 'It is my food and drink to do the will of my Father and to do it until I have completed it.'

It was his 'food and drink' he said: this was the source of his sense of godly purpose and fulfilment. Seen from this angle, Fursa's image of the yoke is a very relevant one. A yoke turns a mere animal into a man's worker and partner. Thus harnessed, the beast, whether it knows it or not, has gained a purpose in life above and beyond the natural cycle of eating, sleeping and reproducing. When an animal has been yoked and put to work, the field will look different because of it. People will eat because of it. They may survive another year and even grow in number because of it. The beast has left a mark on history. In this way the creature's life has been lifted from the mere animal cycle of birth, life and death. The animal will have made a difference: to its environment, to its master, to his family and community.

Our Celtic ancestors were rural people. Profoundly connected with their physical world, they fully appreciated that humans, too, participate in the natural cycles of birth and death: eating, sleeping and reproducing. However, like the ox that has been harnessed by a master, so the woman or man yoked with the Law of God can now offer their shoulder to a higher purpose and make a difference to their environment, and to the family and community of our Heavenly Master. That is the significance God's yoke offers to anyone who will take it onto their shoulder.

We have already seen that the Celtic peoples understood well that different outcomes are possible in this life. As we now look back through centuries of lives and deaths, history offers us momentary glimpses of the one who penned this prayer and offered his shoulder daily to the Divine Yoke. The outcome of his life stands well out of the ordinary. As we recall Fursa's life in the chapters ahead, we will see just what kind of fruit and fulfilment can flow from a faith that says 'May the yoke of the Law of God be upon this shoulder'.

Day Five

'May the . . . coming of the Holy Spirit [be] on this head'

As he prays these words, we might picture Fursa standing before his God in the manner of his compatriot Aidan, with his feet in the waters of the cold North Sea, his arms outstretched in the Celtic tradition of the 'Cross Vigil'. Fursa's head is not bowed down in prayer but held high, eyes lifted to heaven. At times the ancient Celtic believers did kneel to pray, but they also used the traditional Hebrew posture for prayer – the posture known to Jesus – standing with arms raised.

As Fursa stands praying for the coming of the Holy Spirit we recall that it was as Jesus stood in the waters of the river Jordan that the Holy Spirit came down and rested on his head, in bodily form like a dove.

Perhaps, like other monastic forebears of ours, Fursa used aspects of his physical environment to help him immerse his mind in the moments of Christ's life. His dry-stone cell might have evoked the tomb in which Jesus lay when he had conquered sin on Calvary's Cross and in which he awoke on that morning of resurrection. Perhaps his brother Ultan's mountain retreat spoke to Fursa of that mount on which the Son of Mary was revealed to Peter, James and John as the glorious Son of God, his body radiating the uncreated light of the Divine Nature as heaven and earthly dimensions joined where Jesus stood.

Today we picture Fursa standing on the shoreline as he speaks out his words of prayer. What significance do we find in such a place and posture for prayer? The great vista of the ocean stretching from one's feet to the horizon has a way of setting one's own life in perspective. It evokes the vast sweep of God's time and space. The breaking waves lapping at one's feet are the shifting border between the world of land and the world of sea. Here there is no forgetting that in prayer the Christian stands on the frontier that joins heaven and earth. From a more practical viewpoint, standing in the icy seawater would certainly keep our brother Fursa awake.

Physical environment and posture matter because we are physical. Praying in a chair or on a soft bed can often lead to slumber rather than spiritual energy and alertness. A body knows that sitting or lying down means that it is time to rest. A body standing, by contrast, is a body ready for action.

Neither is Fursa's body turned in on itself as if, hedgehog-like, he is hiding from everything outside himself. By standing Fursa makes himself entirely visible. In this position Fursa's attention is not on his navel, his belly or his hands like his monastic contemporaries in the east following other traditions of prayer. With his eyes lifted to heaven Fursa is looking beyond himself.

Some have spoken of the life of prayer as being a 'conversion of attention'. Though his words will invoke hands, feet, shoulders, heart, eyes, ears and nose, it will be to something beyond himself that Fursa will commit them all. In that sense Fursa's prayer will fix my attention not upon my self but on the God to whom I am giving myself – and to the good of his purpose.

When a Celtic Christian stood with arms outstretched in the ancient Cross Vigil his attention was thereby fixed on the passion and death of Christ, on the sins He bore on the Cross for us and on the life He laid down for us. It was a physical way of lifting the believer's mind to something way beyond himself but to which he is connected by the love of Christ, and the aching of his limbs.

Similarly, Fursa's prayer is concerned with fixing the attention of my whole body on that which is beyond myself; namely Heaven, God, Church and neighbour. It is in that sense a selfless prayer that Fursa invites me to offer.

When Christ stood in the Jordan River and the Holy Spirit rested on his head, the result was an anointing with power to do the works of God and transform the lives of those around Him.

Therefore, it is with such an outward focus and motivation that I will look to heaven and say: 'May the coming of the Holy Spirit be upon this head.'

Day Six

'May the . . . coming of the Holy Spirit [be] on this head'

I have often heard people say that they would believe and walk with Christ if only he would prove himself by some lightning flash or tingling feeling, or if he would over-whelm them with an indisputable display of godlike power. The Messiah himself speaks to this insistence in his Gospel. Firstly the Saviour declares that it is 'wicked and perverse' to ask for such a sign, and that for some not even the public display of the Messiah's resurrection would prove sufficient to win their reluctant attention. But secondly, and in complete contrast, Jesus calls out to anyone who is truly thirsty, and speaks these words of amazing promise: 'Come to me and drink. Out of [your] belly will flow rivers of living water.'

Jesus announces that this experience is there for the asking – if only the hearer is thirsty and sincere in their asking. In Fursa's prayer I am to ask daily for the promised Holy Spirit to remain on my head. Evidently by the time Fursa had this daily prayer inscribed upon his memory, he had drunk of the Holy Spirit long and deeply enough to know that this was the Spirit of whom he wished to drink daily for the rest of his life. Daily, then, I will ask it in the words he has bequeathed us. In this way I will welcome the never-ending change in my living, thinking and feel-ing that the Spirit brings.

Of course, in one sense I have no need to ask the Holy Spirit to come when I have already received him. But a Breastplate Prayer is about clothing myself daily in the armour with which God has equipped me. As the Apostle Paul says 'Let us live up to what we have already attained'.

As I pray with Fursa for God's mystical action on my head I am also reminded that my contact with God is so much more than a matter of words. God is my Heavenly Father and so I may talk with him as a child to a parent. This is what our Saviour taught. However, when the Spirit of God descends upon my head like a dove no words are called for. I must simply offer him my head as his resting place.

The Scriptures say that the Spirit of God is also like anointing oil, which one simply allows to soak into the pores of the skin. According to the Old Testament prophet our God is like a mother hen, gathering her brood under her wing. Therefore, I must allow God to chivvy me and encircle me in order to protect me. God's Spirit is like the wind that fuels and guides great ships on the sea. Likewise, I must therefore allow His Spirit to direct and empower me. The Spirit of Truth is a counsellor, and so I must also learn to listen. Jesus said that the Spirit is like a river flowing through me and giving life. I must therefore learn both to drink and to impart.

In these various ways our God invites us to relate to Him, for every image calls for a different response. The image Fursa has chosen implies a moment of calm stillness and collection: silently being touched on the crown of the head. What might that touch convey? Love? Affirmation? Ownership? Blessing? Anointing? For Christ it was all those things, for the Father said 'Behold my Son with whom I am well pleased.'

This touch implies that there is something to be received. As you pray, then, stand before your Heavenly Father, quiet and expectant, and enjoy the moment of stillness as you echo Fursa's words: 'May the coming of the Holy Spirit [be] on this head.'

Day Seven

'May the . . . coming of the Holy Spirit [be] on this head'

It is in my head that obedience to Christ must now begin. To obey the Saviour means to obey the words of his teaching in the Holy Scriptures. It was part of Fursa's daily life to hold these very words in his head. It was to the Scriptures above all that the Celtic monk devoted the work of his memory.

A portion of Fursa's every day was spent reading the Scriptures aloud and copying them out. It was also part of his daily worship to recite the Scriptures from memory. This is a powerful exercise even today. Every week pupils learned to read and write with Fursa and his brothers as their tutors and the Holy Scriptures as their texts. The first Psalm declares that the man is blessed who meditates on God's Laws day and night. This was the very keynote of Fursa's life.

Yet the words of Prophets, Apostles and of the Word of God himself are not recorded for memory's sake only. They were written to teach the believer what to believe and how to understand the world around us; realities both seen and unseen. These God-breathed words give me the insight and godly values that are to inform my daily decisions. The Apostle Paul wrote that it is only when I permit this 'renewal of my mind' that I will find myself transformed.

Fursa's prayer reminds me today that I must be willing to yield my mind to Christ. If I find a difference between my own opinions and the wisdom of the Lord himself, it is His wisdom that I must prefer.

Jesus told his disciples, 'When the Spirit of Truth comes he will remain with you and remind you of all I have said. He will speak to you for me. He will convict of sin and guilt. He will guide you into all truth.'

This means that both remembering Christ's words in Scripture and following them are matters of heavenly co-operation between the believer's mind and the work of the Holy Spirit. In yielding my head to this Holy Spirit I am really inviting this partnership. I am invoking this experience of divine guidance, offering my memory and the very course of my life to His truth.

Only gradually can I understand the implications of this submission to the counsel of the Holy Spirit. That is why Fursa bids me to invite this action daily.

Heavenly Father, for knowing the truth, for a transformed life, for guidance and the ability to remember Christ's eternal words, 'may the coming of the Holy Spirit [be] on this head.'

Day Eight

'May the . . . coming of the Holy Spirit [be] on this head'

When the Holy Spirit of God wished to speak to the prophet Ezekiel, he said, 'Son of Man, stand up, I want to talk with you.'

When suddenly perceiving the closeness of God, the natural human tendency is to fall to the ground. On the island of Patmos, John the Beloved fell at the Lord's feet as though dead, but Jesus said, 'Don't be afraid, John, I want you to write for me.'

On Lake Galilee Simon Peter fell to his knees before Jesus, but the Saviour said, 'Don't be afraid. I am sending you to catch men for me.'

Some of the ancient Greek and Hebrew words we translate today as worship really refer to this instinctive prostration. Yet when Ezekiel fell face down he heard the voice of God reply, 'Stand up son of man, for I am sending you to speak for me'.

To Ezekiel God wishes to speak man-to-man, head-to-head. In effect he is saying, 'I wish to address you as a man; as a thinking, competent, able and willing person of understanding. I want to say to you something that you can comprehend and act upon. That is why I will speak to you face-to-face: to your mind and understanding.'

If, in the time of Fursa, a king asked a petitioner to stand it was an expression of acceptance. A conversation could now proceed. When a king stands face-to-face with his subject something significant is happening. It is significant that we pray Fursa's prayer standing. This was the Hebrew way, the way of Jesus and the way of the ancient Celtic Christians. So it is that we stand.

If God's words to Ezekiel, John and Peter reflect his heart towards humanity from generation to generation, then we must stand ready to have God's words breathed into our lives. Ezekiel, John and Peter had a special call to receive God's revelation and communicate it to others. Though special, that commissioning reflects the call to every Christian. For each of us is called both to learn and to teach. The call of the Apostolic Faith is both to be disciples and to make disciples.

Fursa's prayer bids me now to ask the Father to grant me the same Spirit that he sent to his Son as he stood in the waters of the Jordan River. This Spirit who anointed and rested on Christ's head sent him into the wilderness and anointed him to make disciples of the broken-hearted, the blind, the bound, the grieving and the wounded.

When I stand alongside Fursa and say, 'Let the coming of the Holy Spirit be on this head,' I must pray it understanding that, as God answers, I too will be sent. This sending will lead me to carry God's love to others in the same condition. Confronted by such needs my prayer will become more urgent. I will repeat this request with greater heart for God to answer me as he answered my brother Fursa, for then my going to others will be anointed with that strength to give help and good news that belongs uniquely to those on whose forehead the Spirit rests.

Day Nine

'[Let] the sign of Christ [be] on this forehead'

When a soldier or a sailor receives his commission he expresses this change by taking on a standard form of dress. This new identity as a member of the forces will also be made visible by the severest of haircuts. Henceforward anyone meeting him will perceive instantly what he is by profession. Even in civilian dress his profession will be instantly public for the haircut on its own is enough to make it visible.

So it was for the Celtic monk, too. His head was distinguished by the severe aspect of a hairline shaved right back to a straight line drawn from ear to ear. This haircut or tonsure stretched the monastic forehead to the crown of the monk's head. This extended forehead made Fursa's profession instantly public information. He was recognizable immediately, not only as belonging to Christ, but as belonging to Christ in a very specific way. It signalled that he lived in a pledged household of Christian brothers, given over to a life of study, manual work, prayer and missionary activity after the manner of Christ's Apostles. That indeed was Fursa's profession.

In the Gospels the Son of God commands every Christian to make their own profession of faith something public: 'He who acknowledges me publicly I will acknowledge before my Father in Heaven', declares the Messiah.

'Those who reject me publicly I will reject before my Father in Heaven.' For the believer and the Saviour, faith is in its essence a matter of mutual solidarity.

Accordingly Fursa's faith is not a private or passive spirituality but a virile and bold faith, proud to wear the name of Christ. He is glad to be known as one who had found his identity in God. Fursa is unashamed: soldierlike, he wears his colours proudly.

We note that as a person, a worker, a pastor and a monk, it is not his relationship with any one church, denomination, diocese or religious order that Fursa invokes to distinguish himself. Indeed such categories would have been meaningless to the people of that time. The sign Fursa invokes speaks of his relationship with Christ.

Often we define our identity by explaining our relationships with others:

- I am a pastor because I shepherd others in the flock of Christ.
- I am a teacher. I teach others.
- I am a manager. I manage others.
- I am a psychologist. I study others' minds.
- I am an accountant. I keep accounts for others.
- I may be a mother, a father, a son or daughter, a husband, a wife, an apprentice or a supervisor.

This aspect of our identity helps explain our place in the fabric of society.

But, away from the land of his birth, in a church with little hierarchy, arriving as a stranger in a band of strangers, marked out by a different way of speech, with no real rank or status to defend him in a foreign land, Fursa had no place in this society's fabric. He had to negotiate that place by how he lived. His sense of identity had to be rooted not in his social circumstances but in his belonging to Christ.

Sometimes we hesitate to be so public with our faith lest inadvertently we identify ourselves with some portion of Church culture or Church history that might give cause for embarrassment. But Fursa's statement is not about subcultures or the history of institutions. What he asks and what he offers is that mutual solidarity with Christ of which his faith consists. I must be sure not to offer less when I pray with Fursa: '[Let] the sign of Christ [be] on this forehead.'

Day Ten

'[Let] the sign of Christ [be] on this forehead'

Of what do you conceive when you hear 'the sign of Christ'? The waters of baptism? The sign of the cross, in ash or in oil on the penitent's forehead? More fundamentally, what is brought to mind by the word 'Christ'?

In our day, 'Christ-like' suggests quiet, meek, gentle, harmless and tranquil. This is where 'Christlike' seems to sit in contemporary English language.

However, for the Celtic believer 'Christ' was a word that bristled with strength. What our Celtic fathers heard more clearly than us is that 'Christ' means 'Messiah'. To be Messiah-like means to have a God-given power to save lives and change history; king-like to lead others and bring hope; to raise a standard to fight and prevail for the cause of God. This is the sign Fursa now wants on his forehead. He is praying for a strength that comes not from man but only from heaven, an ability to bring change and mobilize others in campaigning for the Kingdom of God.

Fursa did all of those things. Through the years of his ministry Fursa recruited and led many people into the rigours of monastic community life and to the demands of missionary activity that spanned three continents. All of his biographers attest that Fursa's ministry brought healing, deliverance and salvation to many. This is not a faith of quiet compliance to things that are not the will of God.

It is a bold and virile faith that Fursa's life projects.

Accordingly Fursa's daily prayer is not a tranquil abandonment of self to what-will-be-will-be. Instead he calls out for the Spirit of God to strengthen him with power in his inmost being, as he seeks to obey the apostolic command to 'fight the good fight of the faith'.

In the battles to which any messiah-like believer will be sent – whether the battle against one's own sin and selfishness, or the struggle to do what is good and right in a secular and sinful world; whether the conflicts of family and church life, or the challenges of speaking and showing the grace of God – we need His power.

Whatever the battles were that Fursa envisaged, I believe he daily invokes the power of God in order not to find himself spent or destroyed by them. When the destroying angel was sent to smite the houses of the Hebrews' Egyptian persecutors, that holy sign daubed in blood on the doorposts of the Hebrew houses instructed the avenging angel to pass over so that God's children would not be harmed.

The sign of Christ on our forehead is our Passover signal. Of everyone willing to bear the sign of Christ God says, 'This one is mine,' 'This house is sanctified.' With such an assurance even one caught up in a Messiah's battles can say with the Psalmist, 'In peace I will lie down and sleep, for you alone, Lord, make me dwell in safety.'

You may find yourself pulled in the two directions. At times you may find yourself energized and stirred up –

like a holy warrior who calls to his God for the power to advance and prevail. At other times you may find yourself so vulnerable that you can only hope for the danger to pass you over, as you call out to Christ for his peace and deliverance. Fursa's prayer speaks for both situations and both desires. Whatever your need may be today, you can pray with your Celtic forefather for the sign of Christ – the Messiah's sign – to be on your forehead.

Day 11

'[Let] the hearing of the Holy Spirit [be] in these ears'

In our time we might think of listening to God as being something we do at a level that is internal. We conceive of it as a mental, intuitive or imaginative exercise. Not our older brother Fursa. He offers his ears. It will be through the physical work of hearing and listening that Fursa expects to discern the words of God. This must mean that in the sounds of nature and technology, in the speech of others, in the reading of the Bible or the reciting of memorized verses, Fursa expects somehow to hear the very voice of God. From amid the mixture of this world of sound, Fursa seeks the alertness to recognize those moments when the inspiration and guidance of God are revealing themselves.

To Ezekiel God said, 'Son of man, stand up I wish to speak with you.' In praying with Fursa we echo back this divine desire and say, 'Son of Man I wish to hear you speaking.'

The writer to the Hebrews testifies to God's untiring desire to communicate with human beings. 'In the past God spoke,' he says, 'in many and various ways. But in these last days he has spoken to us by his Son . . . the exact representation of God's being.'

In Fursa's time, long, long before the days of the mass-produced, printed Bible, the Scriptures were still encountered as a collection or library of books. Within that canon of writings, Celtic Christians gravitated especially to the texts of the Gospels and the Psalms, immersing their minds in those inspired words. In order that he might do this, we note that Fursa pledges not his eyes for reading but his ears for hearing.

That is because, for the ancient Celt, the Scriptures were something to be read with the mouth and heard by the ears. Even when reading alone, the believer would speak the sacred words aloud. Sacred reading was not done inwardly in the head. Perhaps in our day we think of silent reading as being cleverer because it is faster. However, the goal of reading Scripture is not to be fast but to let the Scriptures sink deep in our memory and awareness. For the Celtic believer, Scripture reading used hands, eyes, mouth and ears.

So, when Fursa came to Holy Scripture, his ears heard what his mouth spoke. His mouth spoke what his eyes read. His eyes read what the hands of scribes had written. The hands of scribes copied what Apostles had reported. Apostles reported what their ears had heard, their eyes had seen and their hands had touched – as John the Beloved reminds us in his letter.

Through the centuries, many physical faculties have needed to co-operate to bring the word of God to Fursa in the seventh century and to us today. This hearing of God's thoughts is a physical thing indeed.

Whether through this physical relay of sacred communication, or in the conversation of friends and strangers, or in the wordless voices of God's creation, Fursa is praying for the alertness to discern perhaps a certain amplification or insistence in his hearing in those moments when the Spirit of God might be speaking, not to the world or Church at large, but to him alone.

Believer, stand up: the Lord wishes to speak with you.

Day 12

'[Let] the hearing of the Holy Spirit [be] in these ears'

Fursa lived in a world where the presence and voice of God were believed to be experienced within this physical world. We have noted that Fursa does not pray for the hearing of God to be in his mind or in his imagination but rather in his ears. His thinking does not separate alertness to spiritual realities from alertness to the physical world of his senses.

Fursa is remembered by history partly because of the impact among Christians of the stories of Fursa's heavenly visions and revelations. Christians across Europe became aware of them and some of his biographers made much of them, just as in centuries to come curious readers would excite themselves over the visions of Julian of Norwich or Teresa of Avila. But we must not mistake such excitation over things supernatural and imaginative for the spirituality of Fursa himself.

According to the monastic historian Bede, Fursa spoke only rarely of the visions granted him by the Holy Spirit. We know these spiritual encounters were quite real and powerful for Fursa because of the fruit of work that flowed out from them: the establishment of new residential church expressions, which became the monasteries at Killursa on Ireland's west coast, in Norfolk on Britain's east coast, and in the Peronne region in France.

Like every monk, Fursa dedicated a third of his waking hours to reclusion, meaning extended times of solitude with God. This was the source of his energy and impetus in visiting the neighbouring villages and townships to preach the Gospel and set people free from evil spirits.

Fursa later told those who came to him for spiritual direction that he entered upon this ministry in his successive locations in obedience to words spoken to him directly in the way of the Apostles of old. These words of commission, he said, were angelic. By this Fursa meant that he discerned these words with his physical ears. To today's reader such an assertion is startling, but not to the Celtic mind: their God was immanent. For them the Kingdom of Heaven was truly 'at hand'; not for them the Greek concept of spirit and matter being immiscible. Their faith was rooted in the Word that came to earth, became flesh to be touched and handled, and dwelt among us. The Celtic vision was one profoundly at home with the reality of God's material incarnation. Their God was not impossibly distant and removed from the world of His making for as the Apostle Paul said it is in God 'that we all live and move and have our being'.

When teaching seekers of God to find the presence and voice of God for themselves, our Celtic ancestors often spoke of 'tuning the five-stringed lyre'. If you have not guessed it, the five strings stand for our natural senses. The Celtic Christians believed that, properly tuned, our physical senses had the power to attune us to the music and voice of God.

Now, our physical senses are the gifts God has given that connect us with the present moment. So while the thoughts of my mind and the emotions of my heart may connect me with remembered past, interpreted present and imagined future, my physical senses report to me what is around, upon and within me right now.

By touch I feel what is around me at this instant. By sight I perceive what surrounds me at this very moment. I am aware by hearing what is happening in the environment around me as I sit here. Thus my senses attach me to and plant me in the stuff of the present moment. In the past, I was. In the future, I will be. But the present moment is ultimately the only place where I myself truly am. That is why it is only in this moment that I can truly encounter the great 'I am'. If my senses can bring my attention and consciousness more thoroughly into this present moment then, of course, they can help me in my encounter with God.

Therefore as you take your stand before God take some time to tune your five strings. Let yourself become gradually aware of all that your physical senses are reporting to you. As you do this you will find your mood becomes calmed and your alertness heightened. However, enjoy this exercise not merely for the enlivening and refreshing feeling it can bring, but chiefly because it brings your attention back to the present moment, and back to your physical body. Your body, says Scripture, is the Temple of God – the place in which your spirit and the Holy Spirit meet and testify to one another.

'[Let] the hearing of the Holy Spirit [be] in these ears.'

Day 13

'[Let] the hearing of the Holy Spirit [be] in these ears'

The lyre has been used since the most ancient times in the praise of God. A lyre can produce a single note or a chord. It can also sound any number of chords.

The resonance of the instrument is such that, if one lyre is fingered to sound an E major chord and strummed, every other lyre near it will respond. Every string that matches a note in that first lyre's chord will begin to resound – untouched by human hand. Thus something of that first chord passes on invisibly from instrument to instrument.

If a player fingers a second lyre for an E major chord, he need not strum the chord at all. The sound of the chord itself emanating from that first lyre will repeat itself entirely in the second instrument as the invisible beating of the airwaves causes them to resonate without even touching.

This is how it is in the communion of saints. The divine musician has set me up for the worship of God in a certain way. My nature and calling are to do certain works; to render a particular kind of service. He prepared me for this chord while I was in my mother's womb, though I may not yet know what that nature and calling is – what the sound of my chord will be.

However, when my physical ears hear the testimony

and deeds of another in the great cloud of witnesses who ran the same kind of race for which God has designed me, my strings will begin to ring. When my physical ears hear the words of those whose testimony calls me to take that same course, something in me will resonate. Every string in me that matches a note in my forebear's calling will ring and reverberate with what feels like a physical buzz. So it is that even though time and space may divide me from my spiritual ancestor, without our ever meeting or touching, their music can be passed on.

That is why it is in hearing the music of others' lives that I will come to learn how I am strung. It is in listening to others that I will hear the call of God.

As I seek God for that sense of calling and purpose, I must listen and take note of who and what makes me buzz with godly fervour. That is why I must learn, as Fursa did, to give to God the attention of my ears and pray, '[Let] the hearing of the Holy Spirit [be] in these ears.'

Day 14

'[Let] the smelling of the Holy Spirit [be] in this nose'

How close must you be to a person before you can smell them? In Fursa's day perhaps a few paces – downwind, you might smell them before you could see them!

It is for closeness to the Divine Presence that Fursa now prays. In later times saints were to write of a wonderful aroma and sweetness sometimes sensed in special moments of mystical union with God. Such experiences would be remembered for a lifetime. Fursa now prays for just such a fragrant sense of fellowship.

Here we are reminded once more that our Celtic forbears believed that God's presence impinged directly on the material world of their senses; that God was immanent and reachable. It was with this in mind that Celtic Christians heard that 'the Kingdom of God is at hand'. At hand. Within reach. Touching our fingertips.

The Psalmist himself declared that neither physical light nor darkness could hide him from the gaze of God, nor could physical space put any distance between him and God's loving presence. The Apostle Paul affirmed that we live and move and have our being 'in Him'. Another ancient Father wrote that God breathes his Spirit 'closer to you than your own breath'.

So, when Fursa prays that his nose may discern this closeness, he is not merely issuing a metaphor. Neither is

he trying to create a feeling or manufacture an experience. Fursa believes this presence is there in reality and
that all he needs to do in order to discern it is to stop and
breathe.

Many monastic teachers within the Eastern Church
taught that if you desire to achieve such a quietness of
spirit that the reality of God's presence begins to confront
you as something real, you should simply stop, sit and
breathe. Then the God who is closer to you than your own
breath will make himself known to your senses.

Fursa and those eastern mystics shared some common
spiritual heritage in the desert Christians of Syria and
Egypt. So it was with that shared hope of mystical union
that Fursa invited his followers to pray with confidence:
'[Let] the smelling of the Holy Spirit [be] in this nose.'

Day 15

'[Let] the smelling of the Holy Spirit [be] in this nose'

Today Fursa invites me to dedicate to God this most sub-jective of my physical senses. A smell is a hard thing to quantify yet we know how powerful and precise a sense it can be. The perfume worn by my mother when I was a nursing infant; the smell of the soap in my primary school washroom; the aroma of the vapour lamp that comforted my cold-ridden childhood head: all powerfully evoke a feeling or memory.

In Fursa's day men and women understood that, as well as preserving feelings and memories, smells could carry important information. Your nose might tell you if this was safe land to walk on or to build on. Smell could protect you against bacteria and pestilence, from poison-ing and contagious illnesses. Subjective this sense might be but it was important to Fursa's generation in detecting dangers that would otherwise go undiscerned. Such dis-cernment of what was bad could occasionally be life saving.

What Fursa wants to discern daily is the presence of the Holy Spirit. In assessing whether the Spirit of God is present in a situation, a conversation, an opportunity, or an idea, it is to this important yet subjective sense that Fursa now turns.

In Jesus' day there were people who were unable to discern the presence of God even when the very incarnation of his Word was standing, flesh and blood before their very eyes. Some of these people were teachers and experts in law. They sought answers to every kind of question only from the objective black-and-whiteness of words on a page: in laws, edicts, etiquette, precedent and protocol. 'There is no precedent for a Messiah from Galilee', they said.

They were the bureaucrats and lawyers and what they wanted was law, cut and dried. They were considerably less comfortable thinking imaginatively or seeking information from their senses. So it was that, as the Divine Presence stood incarnate before their very eyes, they not only failed to discern it but dismissed it. As a Celtic Christian, Fursa strongly believed in the immanence of God in this world and so prays that he, for one, will not miss this great miracle through a lack of sensitivity.

Some have described the path to knowing God as a 'conversion of attention': a waking up to the reality of God, who is permanently there just waiting to be recognized and worshipped. In his letter to the Christians in Rome, the Apostle Paul says that it is the failure to recognize the reality of God that lies at the heart of a society's sin.

A friend once told me that God is like a 24-7 radio station, broadcasting through the airwaves all around the clock. Yet the radio will not detect what is in the air, invisibly all around it, until its power switch is turned on, and I will not hear what is playing through the earpiece or headset until I place it to my ears. The airwaves can be full of music and yet I will never know until I take some action myself in order to tune in.

Fursa had no doubt that the Holy Spirit was there to be discerned and to that task he daily commits this surprising and sometimes overlooked body-part. His prayer calls us to do the same. '[Let] the smelling of the Holy Spirit [be] in this nose.'

Day 16

'[Let] the vision that the people of heaven have [be] in these eyes'

Fursa can see with his physical eyes and reason with his natural mind. Today he prays for something on an altogether different level – but with what consequence in mind? What is the difference he believes such a vision will make?

A nineteenth-century Russian monk once said:

If you knew the sweetness that awaits the souls of the
    just in heaven,
you would be resolved to endure all the sorrows . . .
    [of] this passing life
with gratitude. Even if your very cell were full of
    worms which gnawed
at your flesh throughout your entire life, you would
    endure it all in order
not to lose that heavenly joy which God has prepared
    for those who love Him.

(Seraphim of Sarov)

When I was first ordained I used to take communion to an elderly neighbour who was housebound, blind and nearly deaf. Despite these frailties this lady's demeanour was of great warmth, happiness and calm. One day I ventured to ask my friend the secret of her inner joy. She replied:

When I first lost my sigh I was very anxious. I was confined in an unfamiliar house and that made me uncomfortable. One night, I was standing before the dressing table, getting ready for bed when a bright light filled the room. The light was so bright that even my blind eyes could see the furniture. But brightest of all was a smiling face looking at me with a smile that would melt any heart. I couldn't describe that face to you except to say that I know it was the face of Jesus, full of love as he looked at me. The joy and peace this made me feel have stayed with me from that day to this.

Nothing in my friend's circumstances had changed. She was still blind, deaf, frail and housebound, but to her that heavenly vision had made all the difference.

Through the course of his life Fursa, too, was treated to certain visions. One account of his life depicts him preaching to great crowds about the visions God had granted him. However, the historian Bede's portrait paints a different picture. According to Bede's history Fursa spoke only sparingly of these visions and only in private to sincere seekers of God. What we can be sure of is that the heavenly perspective Fursa gained from these visions galvanized his efforts and strengthened his endurance through the challenges of his long ministry. The visions didn't make the journey any less arduous. It was the perspective they brought him that made all the difference.

In order that I might be prepared for the challenges of my own journey I will pray with Fursa: '[Let] the vision that the people of heaven have [be] in these eyes.'

Day 17

'[Let] the vision that the people of heaven
have [be] in these eyes'

A thousand years after Fursa's time, in a town south-west of Fursa's English domain, another great pastor, Richard Baxter, would memorably say, 'Heaven will more than compensate any loss we suffer to gain it. But nothing could ever compensate the loss of heaven.' Such vision brought that man the courage to endure slander, danger and imprisonment in exchange for the freedom to cling to faith in Christ alone as his hope of heaven. This he believed and this he preached. And he did so fearlessly because of that perspective.

Fursa's world was also one in which the missionary might pay a high price for preaching the promise of heaven through Christ alone. The cost would be determined by the shifting religious landscape among the clan leaders and local kings of the day. Whether the region was under the sway of a regime friendly or hostile to the Gospel could swiftly change with the falling of a local crown. The uncertainties of those dark ages would have paralysed any preacher whose goal was a quiet and easy life. This is why Fursa prays that his life will not be led by whatever the winds of royal fortune might make politic or opportune in that moment. He prays instead that he will be defined and driven by a heavenly vision.

Maybe Fursa is praying for a precise vision of God's will for which he can then labour and that he can strive to bring about on earth. Perhaps his request is for a taste of God's love for all people to fill his own heart as a pastor and evangelist. It may be that what Fursa has in mind is heaven's ability to see beyond the end of time: to the return of Christ to judge the world; to the end of all suffering and injustice. A vision such as that would certainly give a Christian soul courage for the journey of faith.

In the fullness of time Fursa was to be granted exactly those visions during his extended times alone with God, his body stretched out in his cell, immobilized by an apparent fever, lying unconscious to this world. We can only wonder if Fursa knew that such mystical privileges could be granted him when he first made this bold request of God. But what is easy to see from the reports of his peers is that these supernaturally altered perceptions were a powerful motivation to Fursa to continue exerting himself in his work of preaching and planting, with ever greater fervour and faith. It is therefore with a practical outcome in mind, that I can join with him in praying: '[Let] the vision that the people of heaven have [be] in these eyes.'

Day 18

'[Let] the vision that the people of heaven have [be] in these eyes'

Today we know a little of what it was that Fursa saw in the visions that God granted him. Bede recounts the details of one in which Fursa perceived his countrymen to be in danger from four great fires which threatened to devour them. These were the fires of falsehood, covetousness, discord and injustice.

But what was Fursa to do with this image once he had seen it with his own eyes? Was it sufficient that he had seen the danger of these behaviours in order to be forewarned against them? Was this insight given simply to guide the saint in his teaching? What response could he make to this knowledge?

For four generations, Celtic believers had learned to combat sins using a simple strategy. This strategy was first brought to the monastics of Western Europe by the Romanian-born monk John Cassian. 'Contraria, contrariis sanantur', he said in his learned Latin. 'Opposites heal opposites.'

Following this time-tested approach Fursa would have known that falsehood is healed by the holy combination of silence and honest speech. Such a discipline strengthens trust and mutual knowledge. Likewise, covetousness could be healed by a life of chastity and frugality along with the resolute habit of giving away everything that was surplus to subsistence living. Indeed the Celtic monastics were renowned for these disciplines. Discord must be healed by brotherly devotion and the humble habit of always being first to defer to the needs of the other. Injustice is combated by compassion for the poorest and solidarity with the weakest. All these patterns marked the ways of Fursa's little brothers as together they led their life of close community.

So it was that what Fursa saw in his heavenly vision translated itself into codes of conduct for the households he was forming. The behaviour his neighbours saw incarnated by Fursa's communities was the stuff of those 'opposites', which could put out the destructive fires of falsehood, covetousness, discord and injustice. Their group life was a window onto heavenly society, an enclave for the Kingdom of God and a beacon of light for those dark ages.

We can therefore appreciate that when Fursa prays daily for 'the vision that the people of heaven have', he is not asking out of a frivolous desire for spiritual excitation. His goal is to find the best way to run the race, shaking off those sins which so easily ensnare, and helping others to do the same.

With the same goal in mind I too can pray for 'the vision that the people of heaven have [to be] in these eyes'.

Day 19

'[Let] the vision that the people of heaven
have [be] in these eyes'

This line of Fursa's prayer has me approach God with a bold request indeed. Today I am to ask God to enable me to see all things – my own life, the lives of others, the life of the world – differently. It is surely impossible that I should pray these words without expecting God's answer to do far more than merely alter my perspectives in some academic kind of way. If God answers he will surely upset my very understanding of things, overturning my own order of priorities and values.

In the letter to the Romans I am told that it is through seeing things differently – having a 'new mind' – that my whole life will be transformed ('metamorphosed', to use the Apostle Paul's word). In another place the holy Apostle says that if anyone is 'in Christ' he is thereby re-created; 'Behold old things have passed away and new things have come'.

If my mind is truly opened to such a vision, I can fully expect everything about myself to change as a result. What I want in life will be altered, how I choose to live; what I believe, what I will be willing to suffer for and what I will not suffer for; what I consider right or wrong, good or bad.

Such a change of view has to lie at the heart of my ongoing life of repentance, for unless I see things differently why should I live any differently? The motivation will not be there.

Fursa's beliefs and his actions in life reveal his understanding of things to be rooted in the timeless revelation of God. His work is the work of one who sees himself as an ambassador of heaven. In that sense Fursa wants his vision, his culture and allegiance to be heavenly, not earthbound. He is certainly not one to satisfy himself with a parochial worldview that says: 'Because I was born at this place in this time, and was schooled in this way, and grew up in this family, and was brought up in this society, I see things in such and such a way.' No: Fursa's heart, voiced in these words of prayer, bespeaks a longing to be enlightened by God's own wisdom from eternity – spoken through the ages to the prophets of the Old Covenant and, supremely, through the words of Him who came down from heaven. The Messiah's words were spoken to Apostles 600 years before his time, but they were heard and encountered afresh by Fursa with every sunrise vigil. It is in passing on those freshly encountered words to others that our Celtic brother will discharge his call as an ambassador of eternity, speaking timeless truths, transcending every age and culture.

In our day, by contrast, we often try to recreate the Messiah in our own image. We say, 'If Jesus had come today he would surely say something like this . . .' and then we give what truly is our own perspective. But this is no path to God's revelation. If Jesus had been born where

I was born, had been schooled where I was schooled; if he had been raised in my family, grown up in my home town and country and watched and enjoyed all the same television programmes that I watched, then it might be reasonable to expect him to believe exactly what I grew up to believe. But that is simply not what happened. That is not the story of the Word made flesh. The real Messiah, the Jesus Christ of history, was born in Bethlehem and was raised the son of Mary of the Tribe of Judah.

Celtic believers loved to call him that: MacMhuire – the Son of Mary – because that was the story of the Word made flesh. The name rooted their understanding of Christ in time, in history, on earth, in a place, with a family. Heritage, earth, place and family were things of importance to the Celtic mind. Emphasizing their place in Christ's story meant that to the Celts their Saviour was not an idealized concept of divinity, but a real man who was God. The name underlined that their Messiah had come into their flesh-and-blood world. This Christ, the Messiah of history, grew up and lived in Nazareth, then preached throughout Judea, dying and rising again on Calvary Hill in Jerusalem.

The great Prophets of the Old Testament anticipated it, and the Holy Apostles reported it: that the Messiah, Son of God and Son of Mary, came into the world at an appointed time to an appointed place, and to the people on earth gave appointed teachings whose source was not earthly at all but heavenly.

In one place Jesus says 'My Father tells me what to say and how to say it' and in another the Apostle John declares, 'No one has ever seen God but God the One and Only Begotten, who is at the Father's side; He has made him known.'

In that light Fursa now prays. The teaching of Christ was both from heaven and from history. Both points meant that, in Fursa's mind, Christ's revelation was firm and unchanging. With that clarity he daily asks that God's revelation will transform him rather than the other way round.

Likewise, if I am to pray with Fursa, I must pray anticipating a change in myself. I must pray, prepared for familiar and old perspectives, selfish priorities and wrong values to be gradually purged away. I will pray, ready and hoping for a heavenly vision to inspire me henceforward to want what my God and Saviour wants and do what He desires and loves. When this is our motivation we find ourselves truly seeing eye to eye with the very people of heaven.

Day 20

'[Let] the speech of the people of heaven
[be] in this mouth'

As a Celtic monk, Fursa took no vow of silence. Yet he stood in a tradition that placed a high value on the taming of the tongue. The tongue, we are told, is an organ that can be harnessed either for good or for ill. In his epistle James reminds us that out of our mouth can come either blessing or cursing, with the tongue – like a rudder – guiding the very course of our life.

In close community the power of the tongue to bind or fragment relationships becomes quickly apparent. That is why, from the very earliest times, monastic Christians learned to heed the wisdom of Ecclesiastes: 'Say no more than you have to . . . The more you talk, the more likely you are to say something foolish.'

This is why Fursa's brothers and sisters in their religious households on the continent of Europe, were advised by their exemplar Benedict: 'Let leave to speak be seldom given.' Fursa's prayer, however, takes a different tack. Our Celtic exemplar offers no commitment to copious silence. Nor does he offer a prayer for many words. Fursa's desire is for heavenly words.

Heavenly words may be truth bearing or comforting; uplifting and encouraging; illuminating or convicting. Of such words the composer of the Proverb writes: 'Few words, aptly spoken are like apples of gold in settings of silver.' Likewise, the Psalmist rejoices in his God-sent capacity to 'sustain the weary with a word'. It is to the speaking of such words that Fursa now dedicates his mouth.

Fursa's Celtic contemporary, Aidan, was renowned for his habit of always withdrawing early from social gatherings in order to avoid conversations that might draw him into careless speech and chatter. Likewise, Fursa became known for speaking his deepest thoughts only privately and only to penitent souls sincerely seeking God. (Jesus himself taught that pearls are only for those who appreciate them.) In such a way, Fursa sought to make his words apt to the person and apt to the moment, filled with heavenly intent.

No doubt our Celtic forbear must have slipped, as we do from time to time, by speaking in a way that was out of turn or out of sorts, for the Scriptures say the tongue is restless and 'who can tame it?' That is why every day Fursa renews the dedication of his mouth to God. Morning by morning, he prays that a holy purpose may guide him and that words of insight and knowledge may be given through all that he will speak.

It is with a heart set on blessing others that we can truly join with Fursa and pray: '[Let] the speech of the people of heaven [be] in this mouth.'

Day 21

'[Let] the speech of the people of heaven
[be] in this mouth'

Jesus taught us to pray this way; with few words but forceful ones. The prayer that Christ taught comprises words and phrases so memorable and full of meaning that his prayer has spoken for men, women, boys and girls in every generation since.

The Lord's own prayer is a model of the power of brevity, leaving us with seven simple sentences to express the heart of whatever we may need to say. If our prayers are to follow its divine example then perhaps we might not want our words of prayer to be too much like the words of our everyday conversation, lest we fall into a way of praying which, rather than gather meaning, disperses it in the manner which Jesus associated with Gentile patterns of prayer. 'They think they will be heard,' he said, 'because of the multiplicity of their words.' Unlike some of the Celtic Breastplate prayers, Fursa's prayer follows the Saviour's pattern.

When words are few and forceful, they have a power to remain in the memory for a long time. A succinct insult spoken in a moment's vulnerability can leave a wound that time alone can never heal. A word of blessing, love or affirmation spoken to a ready heart can give joy and retain its power to do so for a lifetime. The Scriptures are

BE THOU MY BREASTPLATE

true to life when they say that 'the power of life and death are in the tongue'.

The Messiah's own teachings were often concluded with words that are hard to forget:

· Go therefore and do likewise.
· Now that you know these things you will be blessed if you do them.
· By this people will know that you are my disciples: that you love one another.
· As the Father sent me so I send you.
· Let the children come to me, for the Kingdom belongs to such as these.
· Whatever you did to the least of these my brethren you did to me.
· This is my body given for you. This is my blood of the New Covenant.
· I am the way, the truth and the life.
· I and the Father are One.

As they recorded these memorable phrases, we can gauge that the Lord's disciples learned the art in their turn.

Among other things Fursa was a teacher and was therefore dependent on the memory of his hearers. With such a ministry, learning to speak succinctly with words full of meaning and resonance is a matter of primary importance. That is why Fursa turns his attention to the speech of the people of heaven, praying that what he speaks may be endowed with heavenly content and power.

Fourteen centuries after Fursa's time we can vouch confidently that God listened to our brother's prayer. The very fact that, one-and-a-half millennia later, you and I are meditating together on his words is more than proof enough that God breathed something through Fursa in answer to the words of his prayer: '[May] the speech of the people of God [be] in this mouth.'

Day 22

'[Let] the speech of the people of heaven
[be] in this mouth'

John the Beloved in his island reclusion on Patmos was treated to a sequence of heavenly visions, which he recorded as the book of Revelation. In these reports we hear the speech of martyrs and confessors, elders and angels, along with the voice of the ascended Son of God. The heavenly speech that John reports is prophetic: it calls us to 'hear what the Spirit is saying to the churches'.

The heavenly speech the Apostle describes is full of encouragement too, reassuring the believer that 'those who endure will not be hurt by the second death'. This heavenly speech is also pastoral, calling the believing soul back to its first love for Christ.

Heaven's words are also words of praise, declaring 'Holy, holy, holy is the Lord God Almighty [and] worthy to receive power, wealth, wisdom and strength, honour, glory and praise.' Other heavenly voices call out for God's justice finally to come and hold sway on earth. Heaven's voices join in singing the song of God's great purpose in Christ: 'To purchase for God people from every tribe and language, nation and race, to become a kingdom of priests to serve our God.'

It is to such speech that Fursa now dedicates his mouth. He prays that, while on earth, he might become a speaker of such prophecy, a giver of such encouragement, an advocate for such justice and a declarer of such praise. In short, his prayer is that he too might boldly declare God's great purpose in Christ.

Clearly, if God is to answer his prayer, Fursa cannot live the life of a silent anchorite, speechlessly observing the lives of others from the safe haven of his hermitage. No, when his brothers' courage weakens Fursa must go and use his heavenly speech to sustain them. When injustice needs correcting, Fursa must be ready to speak up. When worshipping hearts are growing cold, Fursa must recall them to their first love and so be the voice of the Spirit to the churches.

Morning by morning, Fursa will make God's purposes in Christ his song, his speech and his motivation. Only such a response will accord with this humble line of prayer. If Fursa allows himself to live in agreement with his prayer, then any stranger who encounters him will quickly gauge what kind of man they have met, knowing that it is 'out of the overflow of the heart [that] the mouth speaks'. That is why, if I pray this prayer with Fursa today, it is really my heart I am offering to God as I make this request of Him: '[Let] the speech of the people of heaven [be] in this mouth.'

Day 23

'[Let] the speech of the people of heaven
[be] in this mouth'

Which people of heaven might Fursa have hoped to emulate in his own speaking as he offered up this request?

Perhaps the great Apostle Paul: in every town, in prison and on trial Paul's speech was always full of Christ's coming and dying and rising again; of his own journey of conversion – his forgiveness and healing and receiving of the Spirit.

Perhaps the great Apostle Peter: full of the Spirit on the day of Pentecost, Peter's bold speech told of Christ's coming and dying and rising again. It affirmed the need for conversion, forgiveness and the gift of the Holy Spirit. On trial he asserted that he must always tell of his own journey too: of all that he had seen and heard.

Maybe Fursa aspires to the speech of the first martyr, Stephen. His final words unfolded the whole story of salvation, from the call of Abraham to the crucifixion of Christ.

Whether on trial or facing death, on a courtroom stand or a speaker's platform, the speech of these heavenly citizens resounds with the chords of a shared story. Fursa's request for the speech of the people of heaven is a prayer that he might join this chorus and know the same apostolic power upon his own words as he recounts the unchanging themes of the great Gospel story.

We know that Fursa's Saxon neighbours loved their sagas, for we still have the texts of their epic tales of toils and danger; stories of demonic temptations and snares – all heroically faced and overcome. The Celtic peoples, too, loved their stories of pilgrimages to foreign lands; accounts of miracles and healings, of fearlessness and God-sent deliverance. Thus by answering with his own story, with its roots in the great testimony of the heroic St Patrick, Fursa could easily woo the attention of any hearer who asked why, from where and how he had come to be here.

But Fursa's aim was always to unfold for his hearers the most powerful saga of all – the pilgrimage of God's own Son: from heaven, to womb, to earth; to a Cross, to a tomb, to the earth; to the sky and, at last, to the right hand side of God's throne in heaven. Here was a saga full of demonic adversaries, miraculous healings and God-sent deliverance – even from death itself. Then, as now, in order to infuse the hearer's imagination with the truth and importance of it all, the preacher must be the supreme story teller.

Six short years before Fursa landed on Anglia's northeast coast, the local king, Redwald, had played host to the Northumbrian king Edwin. Redwald invited a travelling teller of the Christian story – the Bishop Paulinus – to recount to the gathered regents and courtiers the saga of Christ's pilgrimage in the great Gospel Story. Like any king, Edwin was anxious to have God's blessing to secure his kingly reign, and so he listened to this story intently.

At length Edwin consulted his barons and together they compared this new story with the sagas and legends they already knew. One baron spoke decisively and pointed out to Edwin that never before had a saga sought to give light to our own lives and explain ' . . . what went before this short life and what comes after it. If this story gives us new understanding and a better hope it is for our good that we should follow it.'

So convinced, Edwin submitted his life to Christ and opened the kingdom of Northumbria to the Gospel. It was this decision that paved the way for Fursa's compatriot Aidan and his disciples, Wilfrid, Hilda, the brothers Chad and Cedd, and many other monastic missionaries of Fursa's generation. Indeed, Northumbria was destined soon to become the spiritual boiler-room and missionary powerhouse for the British Isles. So heavenly was the speech Paulinus had given that the very course of Britain's history was altered.

Settling, only six years later, not many miles from where all this took place, Fursa would have heard the tale of this pivotal turn of events. He must surely have prayed with the hope of similar fruit in mind as he took his stand before God each day and asked for 'the speech of the people of heaven [to be] in this mouth'.

Day 24

'[Let] the work of the Church of God
[be] in these hands'

As we read these inspiring words, we must be careful not
to miss the obvious but important point: it is his own
hands that Fursa now dedicates. How often we prefer to
offer other people's hands, or the imaginary hands of the
Church corporate. We hear the call of Christ to serve the
needs of others and declare, 'Yes here is something "the
Church" should be doing.' We condescend to agree with
Jesus and say 'If "the Church" would do something about
this, I would support it.' Thus we let the responsibility for
obeying the words of Jesus rest upon the Church corporate. So when Jesus tells us to visit those who are sick or
in prison; or have to dinner the poor and unwanted and
those who cannot return the favour; when his word commands us to clothe the naked, feed the hungry and welcome the foreigner and refugee, we say 'Yes and Amen;
"the Church" should indeed do these things. I would support "the Church" if it did.' We might say such a thing,
believing that our making the suggestion will count as
virtue. We shirk our responsibility, still believing that we
are on God's side.

But such agreement is not true faith. Such faith cannot
save you. We are not saved by sharing an opinion as to
what might help. James makes this point, in his letter to

the churches and he continues by saying: 'Suppose there are brothers or sisters who need clothes and don't have enough to eat. What good is there in you saying to them "God bless you! Keep warm and eat well!" if you don't give them the necessities of life.'

Fursa pledges not his agreement but his hands; not the imaginary hands of the Church-corporate but his own flesh-and-blood hands. In this concrete way Fursa takes personal responsibility for the works demanded by the love of Christ. 'Make no mistake,' said the Apostle John, 'It is the one who does what is right who is righteous.'

This is why history recalls Fursa not as a suggester of great works, but a doer of them. When Fursa read the Scriptures there was no-one in his mind who needed to obey the things commanded before himself; no-one further up the ladder; no abstract conceptualization of the Church corporate. Fursa's church was a household of people who had learned to hear the words of Christ and the Apostles and say: 'Here I am. Send me.' Indeed, Fursa's prayer invites the brothers and sisters of such households of faith to offer their hands daily.

Each morning, through the discipline of this prayer, Fursa stands before God expecting that some new task might be asked of him as he encounters the Apostolic Scriptures afresh.

On first hearing, this line of prayer might sound grand and ambitious: 'the work of the Church of God in my hands'. Now we realize it is really a humble act of self-offering:

the promise of daily obedience to the Lord's teachings. It is with that simplicity of faith that Fursa now
calls me meekly to pray aloud with him: '[May] the
work of the Church of God [be] in these [my] hands.'

Day 25

'[Let] the work of the Church of God [be] in these hands'

The impact of the work of Fursa's hands proved so endur-
ing that after his death many tales began to be spun con-
cerning Fursa's various achievements. Soon the stories
grew well beyond the limits of Fursa's actual history so
that today the scholar must carefully pan fact from the
fiction as it were gold from silt.

Our Celtic brother was even reinvented by one ancient
writer in the role of a diocesan bishop, adding great
weight no doubt to his initiatives in ministry. To be fair,
this may have been a simple error, on that writer's part,
for the word 'bishop' was not used in Fursa's time with the
technical meaning it gained in later times.

In their efforts to magnify Fursa's heroic status, these
writers invented journeys, meetings, family relationships and
acquaintances, as well as various adventures in ministry.
History does not yield much detail on Fursa's life and
evidently the scribes felt the need to elaborate on what
history had to offer.

Yet the most common inaccuracy among Fursa's
hagiographers lay not in what they added but in what
they omitted. For some have neglected to emphasize that
Fursa was far from the heroic loner or the rugged individual. The truth is that everything that Fursa did, he did

as the member of a small, close community or household. Whether in Ireland, Britain or France, the story of Fursa is more truly the story of a whole group of people. Though there were many whose names we do not know, we can name six of this special company: Fursa, Foillan and Ultan who were three blood brothers and Gobban, Dichull and Emilian who were brothers in the Gospel and who shared their lives with Fursa. In that sense when we hear Fursa's name we must be sure to remember that the presence of a group is always implied.

In the Church we speak at times of giving and receiving 'the right hand of fellowship'. This kind of offering of Fursa's hands was essential to the substance of his group-based work because those hands stand as a symbol of relationship. Hands to help, support, comfort, bless, reassure, gesture, guide, beckon, greet and embrace: these are the kind of hands that are needed to hold such a band of brothers together in a life of community and discipleship.

As I now offer my hands, Fursa's story – the story of his groups – invites me to consider with whom I am standing as I pledge to God my service. With whom am I offering to labour in serving the Kingdom of God? Whom will I be supporting, blessing or beckoning in order to see that the Church of God grows and its members remain bound by cords of love and friendship?

Though I may take my stand before God each day as an individual, Fursa's story reminds me that, in pledging my hands, I must expect to labour within the shared context of a group. For that is the very meaning of the word 'church'.

Therefore consider who it is you need to stand with as you ask the Lord that 'the work of the Church of God [be] in these hands'.

Day 26

'[Let] the work of the Church of God
[be] in these hands'

Fursa's adopted country felt isolated in its haven between
the warm North Atlantic and the cold North Sea. One-
and-a-half centuries earlier, the withdrawal of the Roman
Empire to Europe's east had ushered in for Britain an age
of fragmentary invasions and tribal feuding. Now, in
Fursa's day, a new generation of missionaries was arriving
to reconnect Britain's isolated Christians with the wider
world of the Church. In the intervening years, however,
the landscape of this wider world had become strangely
altered. Now the call of fealty was not to the Emperor, firmly
established in his Byzantine Palace. In Christianity's early
days it was the refusal of such an oath that had cost so
many of the martyrs their lives. With the new wave of
missionaries, the call of fealty was to new ecclesiastical
structures: to protocols and chains of command that
stretched to the Mediterranean and to Rome's last vestige
of order and administration, the walled city on the Vatican
Hill. The watchwords of this new world for the churches
were uniformity and order.

In this new day the chief focus was to be on establish-
ing the new infrastructures of parish and diocese rather
than the missionary community or the monastic household. Gone were the old ways of diversity, brotherhood

and the local autonomy of sister churches. Nor were these the only changes. Fursa's peers were shocked to find that even the calculation of Easter itself had been subjected to change. In Fursa's day each local community was still free to choose which calendar to follow, but only 15 years after Fursa's death the Synod of Whitby required all British Christians to submit to the new method of calculation. The decisive argument was that the monastic method of taking the date of Easter directly from the Gospel of John must surely weigh less than the pronouncement of the hierarchy's most senior prelate.

To the Celtic Christians this institutional world of rank and hierarchy was a foreign world indeed, for all these changes in the expression of Church life had taken place while the Celts had faithfully continued in their more primitive expression of Christianity, innocent in their isolation.

Fursa's world was the more primitive world where the strong centre of a region's Christian life was invariably to be found in small, residential forms of church. In his time, the properties farmed by monastic brothers and sisters were not seen as enclosures, shut away from the Church's mission. They were its lifeblood; the very source of its energy and manpower. Fursa's was a world – as Bede reminds us (disapprovingly) – where bishops deferred to the monastic leaders – not vice versa, and where public services of liturgy were performed not at the centre but at the fringe of Christian ministry, often by monastic brothers with a priestly license. Fursa's was a world of small, local communities, bound together not by the cords of institution and protocol, but by the stuff of soul-friendship and a shared family history.

The Apostle Paul, in his letters of Ephesians and Colossians, and the Apostle Peter, in his letter to the diaspora, both lay out their revelation of how the Kingdom of God was to come through the Church of Jesus Christ. This apostolic revelation names the particular relationships that are key to making that vision a reality. Arrestingly, the relationships named are not the hierarchical relationships of institutional life but the relationships of husbands and wives, parents and children, masters and slaves. In the apostolic vision, the Household of God subsisted most authentically in the households of God's people.

This was a vision with roots in the rich testimony of the Jewish way of worship, for in Passover, Sabbath, in teaching and prayer the continuing tradition of the Old Testament centres the liturgy of faith upon households of faith. For Fursa and his generation, protected by their long isolation, this was still the model and the infrastructure of the Christian Church. Even as a team of celibate workers, Fursa's band structured their ministry on households, living together as brothers. As we have seen, two of the brethren were Fursa's own blood brothers Foillan and Ultan, for his was truly a family household.

Historically, it is language that denotes the people-groups we now call Celts. In the language of Fursa's people we still hear the echo of this very human, grass-roots expression of Church life. Words meaning home and hearth, affection and family, brotherhood, sisterhood and soul-friendship; to the Celtic ear these were the words that expressed their way of Church.

Church programmes today often segregate the ages and genders, fragmenting the community of the family: adults into groups for adults, children into Sunday schools, and young people into youth groups. Perhaps Fursa's primitive world shows a better way.

Today as I speak this line of prayer, I will pray for the Church in all its forms; congregation and monastery; institution and brotherhood; hierarchy and family. But to enter Fursa's world and truly pray his prayer means to keep in mind before anything else the church of my own hearth and household, the church of my brothers, sisters and soul friends. Holding them in my heart I will pray: '[Let] the work of the Church of God [be] in these hands.'

Day 27

'[Let] the work of the Church of God
[be] in these hands'

The Apostle Paul wrote, 'He who desires to be an elder desires a noble thing.' Perhaps it is for that kind of nobility that Fursa directs us to pray. Fursa was certainly an elder; a leader in the Church of his day. Perhaps the phrase invokes the idea of Fursa's special contributions as evangelist, monk and pioneer of Christian communities in the England, Ireland and France of the Dark Ages. Perhaps the 'work of the Church of God' referred to the holy service of those who perform the liturgical functions of priest, deacon, acolyte, thurifer, Gospel-bearer in the community's act of worship. Then again this is a prayer Fursa intends to share with many fellow pilgrims – not with specialists only. What, then, is this 'work of the Church of God' into which his prayer calls me to enter?

Once again I must remember to pause and consider the vocabulary chosen by our Celtic forbears to describe their ancient pattern of church-life: 'family', 'kindred', 'hearth', 'home', 'household' and 'tribe'. What then might it mean to do 'the work of the tribe of God'? For Fursa the special work of his tribe was farming, praying, reading, writing, journeying and preaching.

How might we answer more generally? If we conceive of the Church as being the family of God, exactly what is the work of a family? Surely the work of a family is to make its members secure with a feeling of acceptance and belonging – the experience the Apostle Paul describes as being 'rooted and grounded in love'. It is to give its members both a warm shelter from the world and the courage to enter and engage with the world; to watch over their 'goings out' and 'comings in'. It is to care sufficiently for every member to enable each one to grow up healthy and wise but without smothering or coddling, so that each member is also prepared and ready to take responsibility for the jobs of work that life in this world requires. By praying Fursa's prayer, the one speaking is taking up the responsibility to safeguard the family's welfare by serving those needs.

In Fursa's day it was common for the pioneer of a monastic community to be entrusted with young teenagers to staff his missionary endeavour. This familial, fatherly mentality was therefore essential to Fursa in turning his bands of recruits into the strong and productive communities that they became under his leadership.

So it was with this paternal heart that Fursa undertook the work of the groups of God under his care. Note that Fursa prays daily for his Heavenly Father to continue to entrust him with this practical labour of love, never taking for granted that what was asked of him yesterday will be asked of him today.

This act of repetition tells us a great deal about this man of God. It shows us that the pattern he adopted of the elder serving the younger was an employment that Fursa counted a privilege. Carefully he crafted and modelled his pattern on the disciple-making of the Lord Jesus, who himself declared that he had come into the world 'not to be served but to serve'. This is the understanding that Fursa now expresses in his words of prayer.

If you have a family, kindred, hearth or tribe, praying Fursa's prayer will require you to become its servant as you echo his heartfelt words: '[Let] the work of the Church of God [be] in these hands.'

Day 28

'[Let] the work of the Church of God
[be] in these hands'

Fursa does not say 'on these lips'. How often Christians have seen themselves as heralds of God's kingdom only, announcing its presence, rather than as workers of God's kingdom bringing it into our world by God-given works. The Apostle Paul reminds us 'The Kingdom of God is not a matter of words . . .' What then is this work for our hands?

Hands speak of helping others; helping the least in order to help Christ. This is Jesus' call in Matthew 25. Hands speak also of hospitality and healing. Saint Luke the Physician shows us in his Gospel (the tenth chapter) that it is when we have blessed, dined with, and brought healing to a person's life that we can turn to them and truly say, 'The Kingdom of God has come to you.'

It is with the 'finger of God' that Jesus declares deliverance from evil spirits to be achieved. 'If it is by the finger of God that I cast out unclean spirits,' he said 'then the Kingdom of God has come upon you.' God's hand truly sets people free.

Hands speak of giving. The same Gospel reminds us that it is as we give to others that God will give to us. Hands speak also of praying; praying for others. 'I would that all men everywhere lift up holy hands for kings and rulers,' says the great Apostle. He means lift up 'in prayer'. For Fursa, these activities of hospitality, healing, helping, deliverance, giving and praying were all of a piece. All were elements of his life in community.

Since the physical life of his communities depended on farming, Fursa's hands also had to be set to ploughs, scythes, harnesses, yokes; to milking, flaying, tanning, and threshing – all the work of a monk's hands. The shelters in which Fursa and his brethren lived called upon hands to be put to building, with stone, thatch, timber, wattle and daub and, when money was sufficient, with hammer and nails. A monk of the dark ages was no soft-skinned aesthete, sheltered away with his books. A brother in a Celtic monastery was a worker. So the hands that were laid on the sick, or that distributed alms to the poor; the hands that anointed, invoked the blessing of God or cast out evil spirits; the hands that handled holy books, copied the sacred words of Scripture and lifted themselves to God in prayer; these were the heavy, rough-cast hands of a working man.

Do not think that Fursa's prayer is given to invoke a gentle life of ease; of comfortable, abstract contemplation. Don't have that idea in mind when you pray it. Rather have in mind what practical thing God might have you do today. '[Let] the work of the Church of God [be] in [your] hands.'

Day 29

'[Let] the work of the Church of God
[be] in these hands'

Fursa's prayer directs me to make myself relevant to the work of God. Today I am to ask God to entrust me with the Church-building work of God's choosing.

This was Fursa's prayer, and in time he was to gather pledged communities of soul-friends, working together to spread the knowledge of Christ's Gospel and to build the Tribe of God. This was what happened wherever Fursa went – Ireland, England, France. These things happened because God repeatedly answered Fursa's prayer. In this we must be sure to note that it was God of whom Fursa asked this holy privilege. And it was God who gave it.

Six hundred years after Fursa's passing in AD 650, the pen of a more institutionally minded writer carefully redrafted the story of Fursa's life. This Reinvented-Fursa was said to have been selected, trained, ordained and licensed by his very own great-uncle – none other than the famous Saint Brendan whose venerable authority was beyond any question or doubt. This blood relationship implied that Reinvented-Fursa was also a very junior relation of the local king. Here was a very legitimate Fursa indeed, neatly fitting in to the authenticating structures of the twelfth-century Establishment. Reinvented-Fursa was a fine, obedient citizen, compliantly following orders in meek subjection to the political chain of command of Church and State. Thus it was that the revisionist writer co-opted our pioneering friend, making him appear to endorse a particular pecking order among bishops feuding for power some six centuries after his time. This sanitized 'Saint Fursa of the Holy Establishment' bore scant relation to the bold, radical, Gospel-loving Fursa of history; that self-starting Celtic pioneer of the seventh century.

Our Fursa, the Fursa of history, had a simpler mindset by far. He took his holy orders directly from his God and set himself to doing precisely what the Holy Spirit asked of him – just as Bede later recalled – preaching and plant- ing 'wherever an opportunity should offer'.

Jesus once answered some famous detractors who felt disturbed by the Saviour's own boldness in acting outside the Jerusalem Temple's chain of human command. He said, 'John's power to baptize – was it given by God or man?' No-one accused Jesus of making a false dichotomy. The answer was clear.

Likewise, Fursa looked to God to entrust him directly with opportunities of divine giving. His prayer teaches us to do the same. It is directly to God that I must declare my desire to be a mere spectator of His works no longer, because, as the Scripture says, it is He who prepares in advance the works for me to walk in. It is to God, there- fore, that Fursa has me address these sacred words: '[Let] the work of the Church of God be in these [my] hands.'

Day 30

'[Let] the good of God and of neighbour
[be] in these feet'

In this phrase, Fursa binds together the Divine Good and the common good. His vision of goodness, here, is profoundly rooted in the teaching of the Saviour, who, when asked for the most important command in the Jewish law, replied: 'You must love the Lord your God with all your heart, soul, mind and strength, and your neighbour as yourself.'

Jesus was asked for one but answered with two commands, because neither command is truly fulfilled unless both are fulfilled. Because of this, the letter of James refuses to honour with the name 'faith' any spirituality that fails to express itself in works of love towards ones neighbour. With the same understanding, the Apostle John declares anyone claiming 'love for God' while failing to love his brethren to be a liar. So Fursa is in good company in binding these two 'goods' together. Through history, the name of Christ has been too often injured by Christians who try and separate out these two 'goods'.

And Fursa is very practical. His implication is that whether I am to bless family, friends, colleagues or strangers will depend entirely on where my feet take me. Will my feet take me to the hospital to comfort the suffering friend or acquaintance? Might my feet take me to the charity shop, to the post office, or to the railway arches to give clothes to the naked? Will my feet walk me to my neighbour who might otherwise spend another day without company? Will they take me to a meeting place where relationships can build and conversations deepen?

In Fursa's day, men and women noted the habits of the Celtic evangelists. It was said of Aidan, Fursa's brother in the ministry, that he never travelled by horse, preferring always to journey by foot. He was provided with horses but gave them away because he so valued the opportunities created by travelling by foot. This was the way of the Celtic Apostles. It is as relevant in this century as it was in the seventh.

For myself, I can testify that, even in the noise and rush of the crowded streets of London, I have found myself in conversation, evangelistic, pastoral and hopefully prophetic, with strangers who have stopped me to ask for prayer or a blessing, having seen me in priestly or monastic-looking garb. This treasuring of the face-to-face encounter made possible by a journey on foot was a mark of the evangelists of Fursa's day.

With this frame of mind, Fursa would let his feet stop him at times in order to slow that spontaneous greeting or contact with a friend or stranger, noble or poor man; to slow it right down to the point where a longer or deeper conversation could happen, with all the possibilities that might flow out of that.

At times Fursa's feet would take a detour in order to prolong the opportunity for words of Gospel truth, brotherly encouragement or admonition, or of priestly absolution to flow into a chance encounter. Consider: where do your feet take you from day to day and from week to week, and at what speed do they carry you?

Both factors will be altered if you truly '[let] the good of God and of neighbour [be] in these [your] feet'.

Day 31

'[Let] the good of God and of neighbour
[be] in these feet'

Jesus Christ referred to his own teaching as the 'narrow way'. It is often the harder path because it calls us to live in a way that looks beyond ourselves. The Gospel stretches us beyond a life wrapped up in self; beyond what is familiar, easy and comfortable. For Fursa this stretching meant a journey from home and kindred to a whole new world of challenges.

For the good of God and of neighbour, in AD 633 Fursa's feet took him from the furthest west of Ireland to the furthest east of Britain, where he was to build a community of monastic workers among the Saxon and Anglian peoples of that region. The tie of the Celtic peoples to their native lands was strong and settled. They belonged to their place and it to them. So to live in perpetual exile was seen by Celts as so great a hardship that surely only the most saintly could endure it. Certainly for anyone to migrate as Fursa did was then a more costly choice than now. Yet Fursa's expatriate life would give him an experience in common with his new Anglian and Saxon neighbours whose great-grandparents had made the crossing of the icy North Sea in order to establish their families in Britain.

When the Holy Spirit nudges us onto new and unfamiliar territory our life of prayer becomes more urgent because of it. The surest way to lose any sense of urgency in prayer is simply to have no needs. It is when we are out of our depth and beyond our own resources that we tend to turn to God with the fervent prayer of total dependency.

How fervently Fursa and his little brothers must have prayed as their feet took them uneasily through territories riven by violent crime and tribal warfare. Fursa had left behind him in Ireland a busy and settled ministry to the many who congregated from week to week at his chapel and households in Galway. Now he was in a country foreign in speech and customs, his crowds and congregations replaced by small communities of strangers. With new linguistic challenges to overcome, the manner and pattern of life of Fursa and the brothers would have been scrutinized more than ever before as his pagan neighbours weighed up the character and motives of these monastic latecomers.

How fervently our Celtic brother must have thanked God when he obtained a lease on some Crown land in a Saxon settlement, secreted between dense woodland and the sea at Cnobheresburg. Next came the challenge of locating and fetching stone, then mustering his engineering skills to build the first dry stone cells for his little community – and all under the suspicious eye of his strange new neighbours.

Had Fursa been led only by his own good and wellbeing, his feet might well have returned him swiftly to the warm familiarity of his congregation at Killursa. But that community was well established and Ireland was full of zealous workers for Christ. It was Britain, now empty of civilizing Roman influence, now reverting to its pagan roots, which most needed his apostolic ministry. Indeed Fursa had taken his little band to a part of Britain renowned for its immersion in the darkness of the old ways, which had held all in their sway before the first Christian missionaries had arrived. What better to deepen Fursa's dependence on God than a many-layered challenge such as this!

What if, like Fursa, I will allow my decisions to be guided less by comfort and convenience, less by the eradication of all my own needs and more by what is needed by others, elsewhere? Then, like Fursa, I will soon find myself scrutinized and suspected and operating at the very edge of my abilities. In such moments my prayer will become most truly itself. For the words 'to pray', whether spoken in Greek or Hebrew, Gaelic or Anglo-Saxon, means 'to beg'.

If I learn from Fursa's story I will understand that I am truly asking for discomfort, unease and utter dependence on the goodness of God to equip me if I share his daily prayer and ask that 'the good of God and of neighbour be in [my] feet'!

Day 32

'[Let] the good of God and of neighbour
[be] in these feet'

Today, as in Fursa's day, it is often the moving and going of our brothers and sisters that we celebrate as signs of great faith. 'What faith,' we say, 'of Fursa to journey in those days all those miles from Ireland to England and from England to France.' To be sure, travel was an uncertain and dangerous affair in those dark ages. Indeed it was on a journey in France that Fursa took his final steps on earth. Journeying truly did take some faith.

However, it is often in the not going; the staying and persisting that faith most strongly proves its mettle. God has given us feet to go and feet to stay. Often it will be the good of God and of neighbour that will call us not to leave but to stay.

In Luke's Gospel, Jesus tells his apostolic band to stay with any people who will welcome them, and to remain eating and drinking with them, serving their needs and teaching the Gospel. Fursa did this. At Cnobheresburg, he stayed a full ten years, building Christian communities near what is now called Burgh Castle on Britain's Norfolk coast. He may have stayed even longer at Killursa in Ireland, pioneering his first communities and drawing great congregations to his chapels before he turned his back to Ireland and made his bold crossing to England.

Had he not persisted in working the soils of these two places for so long a portion of his life we might never have heard of Fursa, for his fruit took time to show itself.

It is in their nature that pioneers are always wanting to start things. However, going and beginning is the easy part. The apostolic pioneer must also stay a while in order to lay a solid foundation for his or her work. Therein lies the faithfulness of an apostolic faith. Faithful as he was, Fursa stayed.

Once in Britain, and away from the crowds who attended his chapels in Ireland, Fursa set his emphasis afresh on making disciples through community and teaching face-to-face. This relational focus would have meant that Fursa's hope for lasting fruit was generally invested in a very few people at a time. To persist with his few would have taken a good deal of faith – especially in those inevitable moments when the youth and immaturity of his teenage companions promised to exasperate him.

Weekly, Fursa sought to persuade his pagan neighbours to give up familiar ways and beliefs in exchange for the new and unfamiliar notions of the Gospel of Christ. Such work requires a faith ready to bear with frustrations before fruit and disappointments before reward. Fursa's was a faith that persisted for the long term, and for the good of his neighbours.

Something else bounded Fursa's circle of influence, too. As Fursa continued in his ministry, he came to lay ever greater emphasis on his times of reclusion away from the community, spending progressively more of his time each week alone in his secret cell, given over to contemplation and conversation with God. This rhythm of life meant that Fursa's time in conversation with people had to be even more selectively chosen. Again, such a strategy calls for faith: faith that these fewer encounters would in due time bear fruit, whether pastorally or evangelistically. In that sense, Fursa's twofold emphasis on relational ministry and extended times of solitary prayer limited his constituency. Staying so long in one place at a time also limited the scope of Fursa's immediate impact. But stay he did, for the good of God and of neighbour.

We can all be tempted – whether by the excitement of the new, or boredom with the old, or the simple dread of the day-to-day duties of life and faith – towards a rhythm of life that runs too swiftly from one activity to another, or from one physical or social environment to the next. That is why it is most especially at those times when our feet are itchy that we need to pray soberly with Fursa that our moving and our staying will always be determined by a self-less motivation, in other words that 'the good of God and of neighbour' may instruct our feet.

Day 33

'May the Holy Spirit dwell in this heart'

The ancient Celts loved the Psalms. They resonated with the earthy emotionality of the Psalms, their sense of poetry and the broad scope of them, embracing every human hope and fear. The Psalms were often the first literature that Celtic children learned to read, for the Psalter was always the text the brothers used when teaching the people of their hamlets and villages to read for the first time.

Many of the Hebrew Psalms were forged in times of conflict and battle, producing words of prayer with a deep resonance for the Celtic peoples who lived through the turbulent and violent centuries of the Dark Ages. The Celts also loved penitence as a way of deepening the soul's connection with God, and so the penitential Psalms were a special treasure in the Celts' litany of prayers. It is small surprise, therefore, that Fursa's prayer echoes the prayer of King David in the most famous penitential Psalm of all:

Restore to me the joy of your salvation.
Make my spirit true and steadfast once more.
Do not cast me from your presence,
Or take your Holy Spirit from me.

It is in this moment of humility that Sacred Scripture speaks the name of the Spirit of God for the very first time: the 'Holy Spirit'. In the same way that David asks God not to take away his Holy Spirit, Fursa prays for the Holy Spirit to dwell. This word means not only to live but to remain.

Like the royal psalmist, Fursa makes no assumption that because he connected with the Holy Spirit yesterday it will happen automatically today. Indeed the Son of God himself said: 'I will remain in you if you remain in me.' Of course Christ's desire to remain with us is a steadfast desire. It is our spirits that must be made true and steadfast, for our hearts are naturally fickle. That is why Fursa offers his heart daily.

It is 'through faith' says Apostle Paul that the Holy Spirit dwells in our hearts. Fursa renews that faith daily in this repeated act of self-offering.

'You remain in me,' says the Son of Mary, 'if my words remain in you.' It is precisely in order to incarnate those words Fursa offers his head, forehead, eyes, ears, hands, feet and heart; daily renewing his obedience and love for his Saviour. It is good that Fursa's Breastplate requires me to renew these things daily because without my deliberate attention my natural tendency is to forget anything that lies beyond myself.

A life of selfishness is certainly easier than to continue steadfast in grace and godly fervour. It is surely easier to yield to temptation than it is to resist. It is easier, for instance, to want payback for wrongs than it is to forgive a person from the heart. It is certainly easier to continue unchanged than to repent; to give up rather than to persist in prayer; easier to doubt than to believe; easier to let my mind wander from day to day than to hold in my mind the life, the cross, the resurrection and the love of Christ. In those and other ways Christ's is the harder choice and the narrower way.

That is why my Heavenly Father has set me among brothers and sisters in the faith, and why in his Scripture he has commanded us to 'encourage one another daily' and 'spur one another on to love and good deeds'. Because every believer needs this spurring and encouragement, such soul-friendship is essential to our staying the course to the very end of our pilgrimage. That is why the ancient Celts often repeated the saying: 'colainn gan cheann duine gan anamchara', which means 'the man without a soul-friend is like a body without a head'. Fursa's own pattern of disciple-making, so centred on brotherhood, household and close community, was founded on this understanding.

We might be surprised, then, that one so rooted in the life of community should have bequeathed us a prayer to be prayed by individuals. However, the truth is that no matter how much my brothers and sisters might bless me and keep me, spur me and encourage me, they can never believe for me, for only I can open my own heart to God. Only I can admit his Spirit into my heart by believing. Only I can open that door.

So, although by faith I stand united with the family of God, and although united in intention I pray this line with

Fursa, ultimately I must stand before God as an individual and simply ask on my own behalf that 'the Holy Spirit dwell in this [my] heart.'

Day 34

'May the Holy Spirit dwell in this heart'

The Son of God taught us saying: 'If you love me, keep my commandments and I will pray the Father that he may give you another comforter, the Spirit of truth, who will remain with you forever.'

From these words it follows that, when I pray for the Holy Spirit to dwell in my heart, I am joining my prayer with that of Christ himself. The Lord gives just one condition for my part: that I love him and keep his commandments. This may sound like two conditions but, as the Gospels make clear, the two conditions are truly one and the same.

How then can I know if this prayer has been answered? What evidence can I expect? Holy Scripture makes many references to the signs of the Spirit's presence in a person's heart.

By giving his Spirit God pours his love into our hearts, and testifies to our spirits that we are children of God. The believer will recognize the Spirit's presence deep within their heart or spirit. In other words the believer will feel it inside. These promises were written to the first Christians in Rome.

With his presence the Holy Spirit brings a peace that surpasses understanding, a love that is beyond knowledge and an indescribable joy. Again, this is a knowledge in the emotive heart of the believer – meaning that joy, peace and love are all things that we feel. The Apostles Peter and Paul declared this to the Christians in Philippi and all Asia Minor.

To the believers in Galatia, Corinth and Rome the Apostle Paul promises that the indwelling of the Holy Spirit will turn our hearts to goodness, kindness, gentleness and self control and imparts to us spiritual knowledge, wisdom, healing and discernment and groans of prayer that words cannot express. In other words, there are more outward evidences too.

When Fursa offers his heart as a residence for the Holy Spirit he is not thinking of a presence far beyond the realm of sight and touch. In true Celtic fashion he is expecting the heavenly world to have a material effect on the physical world of his senses.

He therefore expects to feel that joy and peace in his heart. He expects to speak and hear such words of wisdom and knowledge. He expects to impart healing to suffering bodies and tormented souls and Bede records for us that such wonderful blessings did indeed mark the ministry of this prayerful man of God as he travelled into the remote villages and hamlets of East Anglia.

To our contemporary ears, the words 'heart' and 'Spirit' may sound symbolic, inward and intangible. But Christ himself said that I may see the effects of the invisible Spirit in the same way that I can physically see the outward effect of the invisible wind. To our ears the 'heart' of our emotions may seem like a symbolic notion – but only until it is breaking or grieving or filled with infatuation. Then the sensation of it is something quite physical.

Our thinking may tend to Greek dualities of ideal versus actuality or spiritual versus physical, or symbolic versus real, but Celtic thought did not. Its vision of things was an altogether more integrated picture. In the Celtic worldview invisible realities and physical realities interweave and overlap, separated by only a hair's breadth.

So when our Celtic brother prays for the Holy Spirit to dwell in his heart, in Fursa's mind he is praying for a reality that one way or another will make itself seen, felt or heard in the physical realm. To enter the world of Fursa's faith I must therefore open my mind to these possibilities as I pray with Fursa today and ask that 'the Holy Spirit may dwell in this [my] heart.'

Day 35

'May the Holy Spirit dwell in this heart'

The heart is the seat of our emotions. At least we conceive of it that way. In this line of his prayer, Fursa echoes the prayer of the Apostle Paul as he intercedes for the Christians in all his churches. He asks that the 'Holy Spirit [might] dwell in [our] hearts through faith.'

In the Gospel of John the Beloved, Jesus promised that the Holy Spirit once imparted to me will be a companion-counsellor, convicting me of sin and guilt, reminding me of the words of Christ and guiding me into all truth. The Apostle Paul adds that the divine Spirit will work in me to do and to desire the things that God desires. He will alter my desires to match what is good, pure, praiseworthy, noble and worthy.

As the Spirit of God works this change in me through-out the course of my earthly life and plants new desires in my human heart I will sometimes become aware of a conflict between those desires that His Spirit has placed within me and those desires that issue from my own cor-rupt thinking. That is why if I look to my heart in moments of decision I will often find myself presented with a choice of desires to follow:

• to being served or to serve;
• to giving in to annoyance or to walking the extra mile;

- to vengeance or to turning the other cheek;
- to cursing or to blessing;
- to disputing or to peacemaking;
- to anger or to forbearance;
- to bearing a grudge or to forgiving;
- to cowardly silence or to declaring my faith in Christ.

Between my will and every wrong desire, the Holy Spirit comes to remind me of those words of life spoken by the Jesus of Scripture. In this way the Spirit aids me in my every waking decision: counselling, reminding, convicting and guiding.

Though much misunderstood, Fursa's monastic forbear, Morgan of Wales (known to posterity as Pelagius and vilified for his clash against the fatalism of St Augustine) was surely on good ground, and certainly spoke for the theology of the Celtic monastics when he emphasized this Gospel promise, believing that in each moment of decision the believer is both commanded and aided by the power of God's grace to make the righteous choice. The believer must take care to choose wisely and be attentive to the Spirit's promptings in those conscious moments of decision. Many times the call of Christ will require me to feel my earthly nature rise up with an emotional reaction and yet still choose soberly the righteous response – the good desire of the Holy Spirit within me.

At times the bad feeling of wanting to avenge may be stronger than the good feeling of wanting to turn the other cheek. But it will be in the choices I make that the better desire will demonstrate its strength. Since everyone is tempted, and tempted daily, I daily need this convicting and guiding Spirit to be at work within me to desire and do the right thing. Daily, then, I will pray for this wonderful grace and counsel. And I can pray, confident that, if the Holy Spirit dwells in my heart, his grace will always be at hand, guiding me to the right choice. 'May the Holy Spirit dwell in this heart.'

Day 36

'And [let] this person belong entirely to God'

In the time before the first Christian missionaries came, the religion of the people of Britain was, like that of many other ancient peoples, dominated by the fear endemic to leading a mortal life. In those ages before modern medicine, fire brigades, police forces, pesticides and flood control, and when a 'ripe old age' was 50, perhaps people had fewer illusions about their mortality. The Celts knew well that life was uncertain. A season could yield a harvest or a crop failure. A woman's labour could augur a decrease as easily as an increase in the family number. A fever could end in health or in death.

In the face of such uncertainty, the pagan religion of the Celts offered the people spells to weave for their protection and charms to wear in the hope of warding away any unseen dangers. Understanding the power of these habits, engrained deep by countless generations, some of the Celtic missionaries sought to offer Christian alternatives to satisfy every old religious impulse. Thus, instead of a charm, the believer would wear a cross. Instead of the memorized words of a pagan incantation, the believer would learn to recite the words of a Christian prayer. It is possible, therefore, that some Celts made such a switch without feeling much comforted and were left to relate to the Christian God bound by the same attitude of fear and insecurity that their pre-Christian ancestors had known before the Gospel came. Indeed some of the early Breastplate Prayers do seem to give voice to something of that fear-filled feeling.

One example is the prayer of Laidcenn. His Breastplate Prayer has the person who prays call on God daily to help and save from plague or enemy, to defend from every evil, to deliver and guard from foul fiends and the darts of foul demons, to deliver and protect from the unseen nails fashioned by foul fiends. And Laidcenn's crafting of his breastplate is almost obsessive in its concern to name every single body part even down to tonsils and toenails, lest the enemy should sneak in through some unnamed crevice.

But Fursa's prayer is one of a great many Celtic prayers that go far beyond this fear-driven, charm-weaving form. Indeed in essence Fursa's Breastplate is not a prayer for protection at all. It is instead a prayer of self-offering. Daily, in detail and with words, Fursa simply does what the Apostle Paul commands in his letter to the Romans: 'Offer your bodies,' he says, 'as a living sacrifice, holy and pleasing to God. This is your acceptable act of worship.'

This is what Fursa's prayer does – body part by body part – thoroughly but not obsessively. And unlike those fear-driven pagan spells and incantations for protection, the motivation behind Fursa's prayer is not fear, but thanksgiving and worship.

The Apostle calls on me to dedicate my body 'in view of His mercy'. In that same letter, the Apostle Paul reminds me exactly what that mercy is. It is that God the Son came to us clothed in humanity, calling people to put themselves right with God by believing in Him. He gave himself freely to save Jews and Gentiles from the powerful effects of sin; to give life to our mortal bodies; to connect our spirits with that of God himself. He ascended so that Spirit might fill our hearts with love and the cry of worship, setting us free from all fear of judgement and death. This, says the Apostle, is God's gift 'to you whom God has called to belong to Christ'.

In view of such great mercy, I will dedicate my body, and I will do so with no specific outcome in mind other than that I might belong entirely to Him. This is my most fundamental act of thanksgiving for all that God has already done. So it is not in fear but in view of all that mercy that I will tell my Saviour today: 'And [let] this person belong entirely to God.'

Day 37

'And [let] this person belong entirely to God'

Fursa belonged entirely to God in a monastic kind of way. He lived a celibate life in the close community of monastery farms. His days were given over to reclusion with God and frugal living, to farming and the apostolic ministry: preaching, teaching, bringing spiritual relief and healing. All these avenues of service are still available to believers today. When those elements are combined we call them 'monastic'. Today new generations of Christians are appropriating those elements of service in fresh ways and new combinations.

Monastic or not, all of us live days that are marked by a sequence of parts; a liturgy of elements:

- waking up, washing, dressing, eating, blessing, travelling, greeting;
- physical work, mental work, talking, listening and thinking;
- reading, writing, gathering supplies, preparing meals;
- keeping house, keeping company, playing, praying, resting and sleeping.

Part of the monastic liturgy of life is to give oneself to one activity at a time and to pause at the boundaries between each part of the day. When a Celtic monk entered or departed a chapel, he would pause and be still for a moment, to sanctify to God what had gone before and what was to come next. I know believers today who observe a similar discipline whenever leaving or re-entering their home – so dedicating to God their goings out and their comings in.

When the Celtic monk paused at the chapel doorway, it was not because chapel time mattered to God and what came before and after did not. For Fursa and his contemporaries every element of the daily liturgy was sacred. They believed that every moment and activity in their lives could be sanctified by the will of God and encircled by the power of His presence. This is the holistic vision we hear echoed in the poems and prayers of those ancient Celtic believers.

The mother nursing her baby, the ploughman turning the earth, the dairyman milking his cattle, the daughter lighting the fire in the kitchen, the father garnering supplies for the family, the son feeding the livestock in the field, the brother copying the Gospel in his cell – all knew that if they gave themselves to their duty and rendered it as service to Christ, giving to their chore – as the Apostle Paul instructed in Colossians – their whole heart and attention, with faith in the One who sees and rewards what is done in secret, then they were working as God's yokefellows and worshippers, charged with all the potential that comes from loving and being loved by God their maker. We know from their prayers that this was the Celtic vision of things. It is exactly that wholeness of self-dedication that makes Fursa's prayer so compelling.

In his prayer and in his story we can easily perceive that Fursa's faith was not one that subtracted him from society, or abstracted him from truly living his life, nor yet distracted him from serving those around him. No; Fursa's faith was one that filled his life with new senses, new meanings and new potentials, and moreover made that life fruitful. That is the essence of Fursa's longing summarized so powerfully in the words of his Breastplate Prayer. Living the whole of our life in self-offering to our maker: that is the way in which Fursa calls us to 'belong entirely to God'.

Day 38

'And [may] this person belong entirely to God'

In the one who prays this Lorica sincerely, Fursa does not want to present God with a monk, or a priest, or deacon or a worker. This prayer offers God a person. Not half a person.

How often I have offered God little bits of myself. 'Lord I give you my Sunday mornings, Tuesday and Friday evenings. I would really like to give you more time but, Lord, I really do need the rest of the week for going to work, quality time with my wife and family or with friends, doing the shopping, and keeping and maintaining the house. Plus I do need just a little time for sleep and rest. Sorry Lord!'

Such a prayer offers God some parcels of my time but not a whole person – not myself. I may pray with this 'parcels' attitude, not out of any half-heartedness towards God but out of a real misunderstanding as to what it is that God wants – as if God only values the activities my culture might label as 'spiritual'. Do I really believe that the only me that God is interested in is 'me in a church group' or 'me at prayer' or 'me in a religious service' or 'me in a Bible study'? Such a piecemeal view of life is not the Gospel vision of things: it is the way of disintegration.

In the Gospel of John we hear Jesus tell the woman at the well that what the Father is seeking is worshippers. If we understand that word rightly we realize that God is seeking people. For a worshipper is a specific kind of person: a person who holds to God, a person who will fall before God and unashamedly bow to Him; a person who will serve Him and fear Him, people who acknowledge their own lowness to God's highness. That kind of person.

If I am to do as the prayer leads me to and give God my person then it is all of me I must dedicate to him. What that does not mean is that I must now remove all the other items from my schedule. Rather it means that the me I offer to God must include the me at work, the me at the shops, the me who keeps house and attends to family and neighbours and does all those other things. That composite is the real me – the real person.

To live the way of disintegration devalues every aspect of my life. It devalues God – by giving him only bits of myself – and devalues family, friends, community, work and rest – by regarding all those things as somehow less than worthy of a holy God's interest and care. Even a cursory reading of Scripture will quickly show me that in truth God values all those things. The God of all things doesn't want me to offer him a week consisting only of activities that I might regard as 'spiritual'. He does not want me to offer him a week with no rest in it, for example. The Lord of the Sabbath values my leisure time, sometimes more than I do.

In fact, taken together, the Scriptures show me that God doesn't want me to give him weeks in which I haven't given time to loving my spouse, or honouring my parents, guarding my children's happiness, trading fairly, settling my bills promptly, engaging compassionately with the wider community, earning my keep and sharing my home with others – especially those of the household of faith. These are all aspects of the blessed life to which God guides us in his Scriptures.

Sometimes an overscheduled church may pressure us to value only the aspects of our lives that serve the corporate agenda. But, informed by his Celtic faith, Fursa reflects in his Breastplate Prayer the true breadth of Biblical spirituality and bids us bring to God the treasure of a whole life – the reality of a whole person.

So, as I pray this closing line of Fursa's prayer, I will bring to God my whole self and all my activity. Of course the Lord may wish to change what I am offering, to fine tune or transform it, but the point is that I will have dedicated it all to Him for his good pleasure. '[Let] this person belong entirely to God.'

Day 39

'And [may] this person belong entirely to God'

To the contemporary mind, praying Fursa's Breastplate may seem like a symbolic act. But although there is that level to it, we can pray it at a quite literal level. If I am to speak holy words it will be my mouth that does the speaking. If I am to visit the sick or sorrowing, it will be my feet that carry me. If I consider the needs of another person, it will be my head that has done some thinking.

The dedication of my body is no add-on to my service of God, because it is with my body that I will serve Him. Without it, I am dead. In short, my act of worship must be physical because I am physical. That is why the Scripture has said that I must offer my body.

According to Fursa's understanding, a person is a body. Offering to God only my mind would be nonsense. To offer him only my soul would in effect be asking to die. It is precisely that mystical overlap of mind, soul, spirit, will and body that makes us living human beings. When some poor survivor, stranded on his desert island etches on his beach the letters SOS – Save Our Souls – his plea is not for his soul only. In fact his desperate desire is to keep body and soul together. He knows that it is the overlap that makes him alive. That is why the promise of God's Spirit in Scripture is to 'give life to our mortal bodies'.

Fursa's prayer intends that mind, body and soul will together be sanctified. This is why he speaks of the head, the heart and the person. By uniting the physical, mental and spiritual Fursa's vision unites faith and action. His call is not just to the passive life of the hermit. As James says in his epistle 'I will show you my faith by what I do.' Solitude with God was therefore just one part of Fursa's way of life.

Yet neither is Fursa's call simply to the business of the activist. For Christ said 'Close the door of your room and pray to your Father who is unseen.'

Fursa's prayer and the example of his way of life unite these two paths and show us a more holistic vision. In him we see a balance of reclusion and social engagement; a balance of the enclosed life of community and the scattered life of the missionary. Fursa's balance of prayer, study and manual work was the simple, daily rhythm of the monastic way of life.

Whatever my situation in life, I too must find such rhythm; balancing my time alone with God and my time in company; my time for work and my time for rest; my time in the Scriptures and my time befriending; my time in close community and my time in wider society. Like Fursa I too must find the right time for letting his Spirit rest on my forehead in silent contemplation and the right time for going and serving the good of God and of neighbour.

Yet Fursa's prayer is not complicated. It trains me in this balance of thinking, simply through inviting me to repeat its words and to allow the balance expressed through its simple, resonant words gradually to soak in to my mind.

I am not required to be clever or sophisticated to use Fursa's Breastplate. If I cannot read well, I will soon be able to memorize the pattern of its poetic cadences. Neither does Fursa's prayer require me to be on a spiritual high or full of devout feeling in order to pray it. Whether as part of an hour of prayer, or a day, or one minute I can pray this prayer and mean it. All that Fursa implicitly requires is that I believe the words I am speaking, that they express something that I wish to say. That agreement is what will make it a true prayer.

Today Fursa bids me simply to repeat his prayer and agree with what I am saying. '[Let] this person belong entirely to God.'

Day 40

'And [may] this person belong entirely to God'

Over the past 40 days we have learned that Fursa was a person who belonged entirely to God in a very specific way. He belonged entirely, because the shape and course of his whole adult life was determined by his purpose as a missionary and monk. But Fursa is the exception that proves the rule, because even such a specialized and dedicated life as his still embraced going out to manual labour and farm work. His pattern of life included feeding and nurturing those in his households, giving time to others, taking time for rest and at times even engaging in trade. Even as a monk, Fursa's vision of the godly life was not a narrow, religious one that valued only 'spiritual' activities.

In this respect, Fursa's Breastplate bears the family traits common to those ancient Celtic poems and prayers that history has preserved. In their writings we find a legacy of clues that the spirituality of the Brythonic-Celtic peoples was a truly integrated one. Their prayers and breastplates invoked that desire for connection with God from waking to sleeping, and we have seen over the past days that the Celtic vision of God was one that truly filled their whole pattern of life – not just parts of it.

That wide vision of a God who encircles every aspect of the believer's life is reflected in many of the Celtic Loricas or Breastplate Prayers. Phrases from Mary Byrne and Eleanor Hull's beautiful hymn 'Be Thou My Vision' ring with those notes as they render another famous Celtic prayer. Phrases like these evoke something of the vision of Celtic Christianity:

> In the day and the night
> Both waking and sleeping
> Thou ever with me
> Thou in me dwelling
> Whatever befall
> Thou my soul's shelter
> Thou my whole armour
> Be Thou my Breastplate

The very image of the breastplate is of a garment that embraces my whole torso, heart, lungs and vitals in order to save my life. It is a very powerful image of what God wants to give me as I commit myself to Him.

At root, whatever my liturgy of life today this belonging entirely must begin first and foremost in my attitude of heart and mind. I must become like a person entirely caught up in adoration of their beloved and as a lover of God I must hold on tightly to that first love.

The Prophet Jeremiah in Scripture tells me to seek God with all my heart. The Apostle John's Revelation tells me to be hot – not cold or lukewarm. The Apostle Paul says I should offer myself to be a living sacrifice. And Jesus, Son of God and Son of Mary, tells me outright to love God with all my heart, soul, mind and strength. I hear Fursa's Breastplate Prayer ring with all those notes when today it bids me to belong entirely to God.

Over the days that we have prayed Fursa's Prayer together we have thought a lot about what it is we are praying and how God might answer. We recalled the words of Jesus in the Gospel of John telling us that the Lord is seeking persons. Let me ask you if today you will make yourself the answer to God's own prayer?

If today your answer is 'yes' then simply take your stand before God – just as you have these past 40 days and pray once again. Pray Fursa's Breastplate, thinking the meaning of each word as you pray it aloud to God. You may feel something as you do, or you may not feel anything in particular. The point is simply that you offer to God soberly and deliberately words that are meant from the heart.

Pray it believing that you have God's attention as you express your faith in the Christ whom Fursa followed; the Christ of the Bible; the loving, teaching, crucified and risen Christ. The Christ who reveals the love of our Heavenly Father by taking away the sins of our life and filling us with His Spirit.

Have in mind a brother or sister strong in their in faith in the risen Christ, whom you will tell about your recent journey. This is so that your belonging to Him is no secret and so that the promise of being acknowledged by the Saviour is assured. Such a confiding also means that in the journey ahead you can share the joys and struggles of it with a godly and wise soul-friend. This kind of Christian fellowship is crucial because a person without such a soul-friend is a body without a head.

Then, having prayed, pause again. Be still for a moment. For this is a threshold moment. Know that what comes after you pray this prayer will be the presentation of daily opportunities to invite God into your waking life and to live in a way that agrees with what you have prayed.

Whenever you are able, speak freely to your Heavenly Father. Speak honestly, openly and in your own words about absolutely everything. For ultimately it is absolutely everything that Fursa intended for us to share with our God when he first penned the words of his wonderful prayer.

Appendices

Appendix 1: Lent with Fursa –
guidelines for a Breastplate study group

Because, with his disciples, Jesus shared so much of his teaching in the context of meals, because in Scripture the meal is a symbol of heavenly fellowship, and because even a Lenten Fast is in essence a sequence of special meals, let me recommend that you centre your Lent group's weekly meeting on a frugal meal of no more than 12 people. The wisdom of this is that a lot of people find it easier to open up in conversation over a meal than when simply sitting eyeball to eyeball. The practicality of eating also helps to regulate the conversation. A size of seven to eight people – certainly no more than 12 – creates an environment where everybody will feel free to speak and participate.

Begin each session with the meal and end by having a member lead the group in praying the Breastplate together. In between the start and finish let the conversation revolve around a sharing of personal reflections flowing out of each individual's use of the chapters of the previous week. Angled that way, the conversation will be accessible to people at every age and stage of faith.

For each session I have listed a few key scriptures relating to the previous week's chapters, and some questions to prompt your group's conversation about the issues raised by the previous seven days of Breastplate praying. Don't feel you have to use all the questions. Pick whichever questions your group finds inspiring or stretching.

Remember that the goal of these times of food, conversation and prayer is to deepen our sense of soul-friendship and to develop our relationship with God in new ways. The aim is for each one to come away from the course a little different because of it.

Session one

(Members will have read days 1–7.)
Matthew 11.28–30; John 4.34–37; John 7.37–39; John 14.23–26.

The Breastplate Prayer offers the Yoke of God to those feeling a hunger for a greater sense of purpose, productivity or fruitfulness, or with an appetite for a closer connection with God. Do you relate to any of these desires?

Fursa's Breastplate Prayer is built on the understanding that a difference can be made by the joining of human and divine action. How do you relate to that idea?

Have you experimented with different places and postures for prayer? If so how do they work for you?

Has Fursa's prayer changed how you think about connecting with the Spirit of God? What are you hoping for as you pray his prayer?

Session two
(Members will have read days 8–14)
Hebrews 1.1–2, 11.35–12.2; Matthew 10.32–33; I Corinthians 8.1; Psalm 46.10

Do you feel that the world of faith and church engages you as a capable adult, or do you sometimes find that you are made to feel less than that? What do you see as a healthy balance?

What does it mean to you to acknowledge Christ publicly? Has this experience been important to you in strengthening your faith?

Why might Christians have lost a messianic sense of confidence since Fursa's time? What might a healthy expression of messianic confidence look like?

Share any experiences of moments when you have felt God was somehow communicating with you personally through Scripture, through others or through your senses. Is Fursa's expectation of these things different from ours?

What in the stories and testimonies of others has made you resonate or 'buzz'?

Session three
(Members will have read days 15–21)
Romans 12.9–21, Hebrews 12.1–3; John 1.14, James 3.2–12

Share any experiences of a sense of spiritual discernment. Why do you think believers sometimes struggle with the more subjective elements of the Christian experience?

Share any ways in which you are finding the Breastplate habit helpful in 'tuning in' to God's presence or in achieving a greater 'conversion of attention'.

What role should a vision of heaven play in our faith and motivations? Is this an area where your thinking is changing?

Do you have a vision of good practice or of Christian living that inspires you? How might we acquire such a vision?

Do you find the name MacMhuire (Son of Mary) a helpful title for Jesus? How can we best guard against re-inventing Jesus in our own image?

How do you relate to the idea of taming the tongue?

Session four
(Members will have read days 22–28)
Colossians 3.16–17; James 3.17, I Thessalonians 2.6–12, Romans 16.1–23

Are there ways in which you could strengthen the mix of encouraging/pastoral/prophetic/evangelistic/praising and storytelling in your conversation?

Have you experienced times when our faith seems to consist more of opinions than actions? How can we guard against a faith that is too theoretical?

The structures of the Church in Fursa's day remind us that there are many different ways of expressing the life of the Church. What different priorities, practices and patterns of Church might we embrace from our glimpse into Fursa's world?

What might it mean for you to be the servant of the church of your hearth, household, brotherhood, sisterhood and soul-friends?

Session five
(Members will have read days 29–35)
John 16.7–15; Ephesians 2.10; Luke 10.5–9; Acts 4.23–21

Are there ways in which we sometimes look to people instead of to God in our search for ways to serve God?

Are the speed at which you live and the places you allow your feet to take you 'live' issues in your service of God and neighbour? What could you change?

Persisting and moving can both be expressions of faith and obedience to the will of God. Which of the two do you find more challenging? Which do you feel is relevant to you today?

Are there ways in which you find Christ's call on the believer to be narrow or difficult?

How do you know if the Holy Spirit is dwelling in your heart? How do you relate to the signs listed on day 34?

Can you share an experience of the Holy Spirit guiding you to the right choice? How did the Lord guide you?

Session six
(Members will have read days 36–40)
Romans 8.11–17; Psalm 139.1–14, Revelation 3.20
Re-read day 40 to the group.

In your relationship with God, do you feel more driven by an attitude of thanksgiving or an attitude of fear?

Think about the liturgy of your day. Are there ways in which you have excluded God from certain parts of your life? Are there ways in which you can more consciously offer each part of your daily life to God?

Pray the Breastplate for one another

You have reached the end of Lent with Fursa. What do you want this threshold moment to mean for you?

Appendix 2:
A weekend with Fursa –
guidelines for a group retreat

Fursa's life of community revolved around a rhythm of times together – eating, talking and working – and times alone with God in solitary prayer. A retreat can follow that same pattern, with the bulk of the time spent in solitary reading and prayer but punctuated by meals and conversation.

Let me recommend a rural retreat in a place where it's easy to relax and become quiet and where you can get out into nature and enjoy solitary walks in God's creation in between your meals and conversations. The testimony of Celtic saints like Aidan and Fursa tells us that ancient Celts liked to pray by the water's edge and on high hills. For a calming and inspiring place to pray, you could try the same.

For each session I have listed a key Scripture text and a starter question to prompt your conversation about the issues raised by what you will have just read and prayed in the previous time alone. Let your conversation in the meals/times together revolve around a sharing of personal reflections flowing out of each individual's reading and praying. Angled that way, the conversation will be accessible to retreatants at every age and stage of faith.

Remember that the goal of such a retreat is to deepen our sense of soul-friendship and to develop our relationship with God in new ways. The aim is for each one to come away from the retreat refreshed and a little different because of it.

Here's a suggestion for a schedule for a gently paced weekend retreat:

FRIDAY EVENING – ARRIVE

REFRESHMENTS/TIME TOGETHER
Pray through the Breastplate together

TIME ALONE
Read and pray through days1–7

REFRESHMENTS/TIME TOGETHER
Matthew 11.28–30

The Breastplate Prayer offers the Yoke of God to those feeling a hunger for a greater sense of purpose, productivity or fruitfulness, or with an appetite for a closer connection with God. Do you relate to any of these desires?

TIME ALONE/BEDTIME
Read and pray through days 8–14

SATURDAY MORNING

BREAKFAST/TIME TOGETHER
Hebrews 1.1–2, 11.35–12.2

BE THOU MY BREASTPLATE

Share any experiences of moments when you have felt
God was somehow communicating with you personally
through Scripture, through the testimony of others, or
through your senses. Is Fursa's expectation of these things
different to ours?

TIME ALONE
Read and pray through days 15–21

MORNING COFFEE/TIME TOGETHER
Romans 12.9–21

Do you find the name MacMhuire (Son of Mary) a helpful
title for Jesus? How can we best guard against re-inventing
Jesus in our own image?

TIME ALONE
Read and pray through days 22–28

LUNCH/TIME TOGETHER
Colossians 3.16–17

How might you strengthen the mix of encouraging/
pastoral/prophetic/evangelistic/praising and story telling
in your conversation?

What might it mean for you to become the servant of
the church of your hearth, household, brotherhood, sisterhood and soul-friends?

TIME ALONE
Read and pray through days 29–35

DINNER/TIME TOGETHER
John 16.7–15

Persisting and moving can both be expressions of faith and obedience to the will of God. Which do you feel is relevant to you today?

How do you know if the Holy Spirit is dwelling in your heart? How do you relate to the signs listed on day 34?

TIME ALONE/BEDTIME
Read and pray through 36–40

SUNDAY MORNING

BREAKFAST/TIME TOGETHER
Romans 8.11–17, Revelation 3.20
Re-read day 40 together

Are there ways in which you have excluded God from certain parts of your life? Are there ways in which you can more consciously offer each part of your daily life to God?

Now pray the Breastplate Prayer for one another.

You have reached the end of Lent with Fursa. Tell each other what you want this threshold moment to mean for you.